THE SALE OF A COUNTRY

Behind the Scenes at the Canada-U.S. Free Trade Negotiations Office

Volume 1

Shelley Ann Clark

To order additional copies of this book, contact:
Xlibris Corporation
1-888-795-4274
www.Xlibris.com
Orders@Xlibris.com
103166

"THE SALE OF A COUNTRY" INDEX

APPENDICES

Dedication

I dedicate this book to my best friend Margaret Bowlby and all Canadian vanguards who feel personally devoted to the preservation of our culture and value system. Margaret Bowlby is a person of integrity and has been a representative of Canadian vanguards for many years. Margaret has worn many hats to assist me with this project, and her devotion and hard work have proven invaluable.

I would also like to take this opportunity to thank my two sons, Stephen and David for all their support. Stephen for providing his editorial skills and David for his technical support. This book became reality due to my two son's understanding of it's importance to Canadians to know the whole truth.

A Special Note of Thanks to John Richard Bowlby for his devotion, his loyalty, his friendship, and his moral support during the long hours he put in as my Campaign Manager during the 1993 Federal Elections. John was also a witness to many of the events that surrounded my expose of the Canada-U.S. Free Trade Agreement. To Charles Frey who agreed to be a key witness to my meeting with the Royal Canadian Mounted Police, Crime Investigations Unit. My heartfelt appreciation and thanks to a very dear, warm-hearted and sensitive friend, Marie Marthe Champagne who has given Margaret and I all the encouragement and support that was essential for us to do our job.

To all of you I say "Thank You" for everything you have done to make this book become a reality and not just a dream.

Shelley Ann Clark

Prologue

One hundred & forty-two {142 } years went by before Canada achieved what everyone thought impossible, a "Free Trade Agreement" with the United States of America; an agreement that became a major historical event for Canada.

Even though it has been 24 years since the infamous Canada-U.S. Free Trade Agreement made history minutes before midnight on October 3, 1987, events over those past 24 years have created a demand for this book to be written. This demand has emanated not only from Canadians, but also from individuals from around the world.

Due to this incredible demand, which took me completely by surprise, I have made the decision to write this book. "THE SALE OF A COUNTRY" is a riveting account of the events that took place behind the scenes in the Canadian Free Trade Office. Deputy Chief Negotiator, Gordon Ritchie wrote "Wrestling with the Elephant" from his point of view and Foreign Affairs Officers, Michael Hart, Bill Dymond and Colin Robertson wrote "Decision at Midnight" from their perspective. They have done an excellent job, but it is an account of the events in which they were participants. There is another side to the story on how we "LOST" our country. Because Germain Denis did everything under a veil of secrecy, none of them knew about the machinations that went on behind the scenes.

My decision was also based on the fact that I wanted to ensure that the whole story of what happened to our country would be known to Canadians and would become part of our historical records. I knew that this would not occur because the mainstream media was not and is still not doing their job. The mainstream media is not working for you.

The mainstream media was completely under the Prime Minister's control. Lord Thompson and Conrad Black who owned all the mainstream media at the time, were close buddies of Brian Mulroney. The more Canadians and I tried to get the mainstream media to carry my story, the more we discovered that Canada no longer had an "independent press". It reminded me of an article written by John Swinton (now deceased), that was passed on to me by a caring Canadian. The article appeared in an American publication titled "The Journalists" in July 1993. A copy of this article can be found in Chapter 20 "The Mainstream Media—THE TRUTH".

I am also reminded of an ancient Russian proverb: "What is written with a pen cannot be removed with a hatchet".

FTA Historical Background

Summarized Historical Background which led to an historical event for Canada on January 2, 1988

1846—The idea of having free trade between countries was first conceived when Britain repealed its Corn Laws and ended preferences enjoyed by Canadian producers in the British market.

In 1866, Sir John A Macdonald is unsuccessful in negotiating a reciprocity agreement with the U.S.

In 1896, Sir Wilfrid Laurier's overtures to the Americans are rejected.

It was not until 1934 that the U.S. is receptive to the idea when the U.S. Congress adopts Reciprocal Trade Agreements with other dominions.

In 1935, Canada and the United States successfully negotiate a trade agreement under the RTA program, ushering in more free trade than under any previous agreement.

1957—Gordon Royal Commission study warns about the high cost of protectionism to the Canadian economy.

1967—A pioneering study of the benefits of free trade between Canada and the U.S.A. is published by the Wonnacott brothers

1975—The Economic Council of Canada recommends Canada negotiate a free trade agreement with the U.S.A.

1982—Senate Foreign Affairs Committee recommends Canada negotiate a free trade agreement with the U.S.A.

1985—On September 26, Prime Minister Brian Mulroney announces that Canada will seek a new trade agreement with the U.S.A.

1985—November 8, Canadian Prime Minister announces the appointment of Simon Reisman as the Chief Trade Negotiator

`1986—On April 10, Simon Reisman, Chief Negotiator for Canada and newly appointed Chief Negotiator for the U.S.A., Peter Murphy, meet for the first time in Washington.

1987—On September 23, Reisman suspends negotiations.

1987—On October 1, at the insistent urging of Canadian Ambassador to the U.S., Alan Gotlieb, U.S. Treasury Secretary James Baker and Clayton Yeutter finally agree that the U.S. could return to the negotiations table to meet fundamental Canadian requirements on trade remedies and dispute settlement. The Prime Minister and the Cabinet agree.

1987—Minutes before midnight on October 3, an outline of the Free Trade Agreement is signed by all parties in Washington.

1988—January 2—Historical Event. Canadian Prime Minister, Brian Mulroney and American President Ronald Reagan make history as they sign the "Free Trade Agreement".

Chapter 1

Simon Reisman's Appointment

When Prime Minister Brian Mulroney made the decision to appoint Simon Reisman to lead the Canadian Team for the Free Trade Negotiations; serious concerns were expressed by many.

Gordon Ritchie, who was appointed by Mulroney as the Deputy Chief Negotiator (2nd in Command at the Canadian Trade Negotiations Office), in his book "Wrestling with the Elephant", (page #57) states: "Our enthusiasm was tempered only by concern that the rules had changed in the decade since Simon had last roamed the upper levels of government. The players had also changed". I believe that what Gordon Ritchie was trying to diplomatically tell us is that the Rules for Playing Political Games had changed since Canadians had voted in Brian Mulroney as our Prime Minister. As you read on, you will see and understand what I mean.

What I found strange at the time and still find strange to this day, is the fact that Brian Mulroney appointed Simon Reisman to lead the Canadian Team. The Prime Minister must have known Simon's reputation; that Simon was not a push over and could not be controlled. In fact, Simon always had a reputation for being stubborn as a mule and to stick to his ideals like a blood sucker sticks to human flesh.

So why did Mulroney insist on appointing Reisman to lead our Canadian Negotiating Team? Most of you who followed the negotiations in the mainstream media would have noticed that near the end of the negotiations, it was always Gordon Ritchie that was the headliner in the news, not Simon Reisman. Reisman had just become a "figure head" as Gordon Ritchie took over and became the media's shining star.

Gordon Ritchie knew how to play the political game. Ritchie knew the players and was extremely at ease in the corridors of power. He is a mixture of being a hard nose and a straight shooter.

I was not surprised at this development. Anyone who is in the know in Ottawa knew Gordon Ritchie had the "brains" and the "stones" to do the job.

Surely, the Prime Minister knew the reputation of both Reisman and Ritchie. By appointing them to lead the Canadian Team he ensured that Canadians would believe that the negotiations were "above-board". Why did the P.M. hire a 3rd unknown negotiator? Because he knew that no one would focus on the 3rd person down the line, one German Denis. The Prime Minister knew that Denis was greedy and that he would be more than willing to do his bidding to put his career on the "political fast track".

The above certainly explains why it was Germain Denis who made clandestine telephone calls to Brian and Brian to him. The orders to delete entire chapters and alter figures in the Premiers Briefing Books must have come from the Prime Minister. Denis would not do this on his own initiative. It was Denis to whom the Prime Minister entrusted these clandestine activities that took place at midnight.

In the end, the only question that remained was put to Gordon Ritchie by Paul Martin Jr. ". . . Is the agreement good for Canada?" This question has remained unanswered for many Canadians, but for some it has been answered; but what a negative development it has been for us Serfs.

Gordon Ritchie, in his book "Wrestling the Elephant" talks about his father's thoughts on the matter of Free Trade. Gordon Ritchie states: . . . . "Edgar Ritchie was wary of Canada drawing too close to the friendly giant, and suffocating in America's embrace."

AN INTRODUCTION TO GERMAIN DENIS

"An Anonymous Gift"

Chapter 2

Who is Germain Denis?

Germain Denis is the man that former Prime Minister Brian Mulroney parachuted into the job as the 3rd highest ranking negotiator at the Canada-U.S. Free Trade Negotiations Office. This occurred during the fall of 1986, several months after the Trade Negotiations Office opened its doors. Why was Denis not appointed by the Prime Minister at the time that he was putting together the people he needed to head up his Canadian team?

Denis was literally parachuted into the job after weeks of complaints by the Francophone community to the mainstream media, that the top jobs at the Trade Negotiations Office (TNO) had only been given to Anglophones. The Francophones made so much noise about this fact that my colleagues at the Trade Negotiations Office were telling me not to be surprised if suddenly, a Francophone was appointed as one of the top 3 negotiators to lead the Canadian Team.

Was this the real reason that Denis was appointed so quickly? Or were these complaints orchestrated by Mulroney and his advisers to justify Denis's appointment? I shall let the reader decide.

If you look up Germain Denis on Cambridge's "Who's Who?", you will find that they recognized him as a VIP Member. They also recognized him for showing dedication, leadership and excellence in international trade consulting.

According to Who's Who, Mr. Denis has 40 years experience as a consultant and in the public sector, with a particular expertise in recent years in world food and feed grain markets. Mr. Denis has served as the Executive Director of the International Grains Council, monitoring international grain trade agreements and food aid conventions, attending conferences with government and industry leaders, analyzing the global supply and demand situation in food and feed grain markets, and promoting measures to enhance the food security of developing countries.

While in the public sector, he contributed to the establishment of the World Trade Organization to support the open, fair and stable trading framework essential for the growth and the realization of sustainable development opportunities around the world.

Mr. Denis earned a Bachelor's degree from the University of Sherbrooke, followed by a Master of Public Administration from Laval University. He has been affiliated with several organizations, including Boston University's African Presidential Archives and Research Center, the Royal Institute of International Affairs, the World Trade Law Association, the British Branch of the International Law Association, and the Institute of Directors for the International Food and Agribusiness Management Association.

All that the reader has read above has been provided by Cambridge Who's Who. What is interesting is what my researcher discovered when she dug further into what Cambridge Who's Who has to offer and sells to individuals.

If you check out the Cambridge Registry and ask for a profile on Germain Denis, you will see that he is the recipient of the following awards: The World Medal of Freedom given out by the American Biographical Institute (2005); Agri-Food Cooperation Medal, awarded by the International Industrial Academy Russia (2003); Alimentos Argentinos, Ordre Merite Agricole, France (1996); Great Minds of the 21st Century Award; **American Medal of Honor**, Merite Professionnel, Bourse de Commerce, Paris.

But if you do a bit more research, you will discover that the very people who praise Germain Denis also offers its clients the opportunity to purchase any award they wish to have. Did Germain Denis purchase his awards? This is the man who shamelessly promotes himself on the internet with awards that he may have purchased. Orders and Awards from the American Biographical Institute and the "Cambridge Who's Who", including the venerable, exclusively U.S. military "Medal of Honor". Was Denis ever in the American military? This medal is reserved to honor their war heroes. Can an alleged non-military Canadian be the recipient of this award?" It certainly begs the question as to whether Denis has purchased his awards. {WIKIPEDIA, an absolute must read on the American Biographical Institute}.

Chapter 3

The Interview

In July 1986, I was walking down the hallway of the Executive Offices at the Department of Foreign Affairs and International Trade {DFAIT} when I ran into an officer I had worked with a few years earlier. As we spoke, she mentioned that DFAIT was opening up a new office to deal with the negotiations for free trade between Canada and the U.S. It was strongly suggested that I should apply for a position there as it would not only be very interesting work, but would definitely be an advantageous move for my career.

On the same day, I met with my Human Resources Officer and asked her to provide the Trade Negotiations Office {TNO} with my name for a job. By the end of the day, I was informed that she had booked an interview for me with the Assistant Deputy Minister for Multilateral Trade, a man by the name of Germain Denis. He was just setting up his office over there and needed someone with my background. When I asked her what my chances were of getting the job, she smiled and said: "Oh! This interview is just a formality—you have the job". This turned out to be true. {Refer to Appendix "B"}

An interview was set up for the very next morning, but not with Germain Denis. This was step one. I met with a Foreign Service Officer who was one of Denis top aides. It was a strange interview as I was not questioned about my areas of expertise nor was I questioned about my availability to do overtime. There were also no questions asked about my employment background. The interview was more of an opportunity to meet with me to tell me I had the job.

Step two came along when I was asked to meet with Denis almost a week later. Again, this was not your usual run-of-the-mill interview. It was not an interview, it was just an opportunity for Denis to meet me. At the end of three (3) minutes, he said, "When can you start?" Wanting this challenging job to advance my career, I agreed to become his Executive Assistant.

I was not advised that I would actually be wearing several hats during my journey with him. As it turned out, I was asked to assist the Deputy Chief Negotiator, Gordon Ritchie, until the person he had hired as his E.A. was made available to be transferred to the TNO and any time she was absent. As no one had yet been hired to head the Hospitality sector, I was asked to take on those responsibilities for several months as well. I was also responsible for organizing and supervising the Team that assembled the 35 negotiating books. On more than one occasion, I was asked to sit in on the negotiations when Simon Reisman's senior officer was absent. This officer was responsible for taking notes and for providing both teams with whatever they required during the negotiations. I was also asked to be part of the team of proofreaders. {Refer to Appendix "A"}

Denis made me responsible for seeing to it that his team met their deadlines. Because Denis was not only the 3rd top free trade negotiator, but was also the Assistant Deputy Minister for Multilateral Trade, this often took him out of the country and therefore left me to pass on his instructions and any explanations required. Over time, I developed a good and solid relationship with his team. At that time, there was mutual respect between his team and me. But later, when I blew the whistle on the FTA, no one came forward, they all seemed to vanish. Simon Reisman, when interviewed by CBC's Peter Czowski, denied that he was even aware of a person by the name of Shelley Ann Clark who had worked at the TNO. He said he did not know any such person and quickly moved on to another topic; how convenient to suddenly become a "phantom" executive so this person could avoid accountability. Without realizing it at the time, in legal terms, I had become "de novo".

By being labeled "de novo" notice how quickly it gave them licence to avoid the issue. {The "de novo" saga continues in Volume II—"FIGHTING SHADOWS"}. What are they afraid of and what were they trying to hide from you?

I became the liaison between the TNO, the Privy Council Office (PCO), the Prime Minister's Office (PMO), all Federal Government departments and Non-governmental Organizations (NGO's).

It became evident, over time, that the conversation that took place in the hallway of the Executive Offices was no coincidence. I had been hand-picked for the job. It was obviously believed that I would do anything to advance my career. How wrong they were. Who are "they"? Germain Denis, who took his orders directly from Prime Minister Brian Mulroney, was allegedly told to make sure that he hired someone who was greedy enough to do anything to move his or her career ahead.

Chapter 4

The Chain of Command

The most blatant and obvious and unusual occurrence that jumped out at me was the fact that in the case of Germain Denis the standard federal government protocol dealing with the CHAIN OF COMMAND was not being respected. This chain of command is in place within every federal department and agency.

The bureaucracy and protocol in the federal government operates within the perimeters of the following pecking order. If the Prime Minister requires information on any subject, he goes to the Federal Cabinet Minister responsible; the Minister goes to his Deputy Minister; the Deputy Minister goes to the Assistant Deputy Minister and the Assistant Deputy Minister goes to his Director General of whatever bureau deals with the issue the Prime Minister was asking about. The Director General then meets with his Directors and asks them to prepare a response for the Prime Minister.

At the Trade Negotiations Office, the Chain of Command should have been as follows: When the Prime Minister needed information or an update on the free trade negotiations he would have asked his top aide, Bernard Roy, to contact either the Cabinet Minister for International Trade or Simon Reisman who was the Ambassador/ Head of the Canadian Negotiating Team. It would follow that Reisman would contact his 2nd in command, Gordon Ritchie and if Ritchie did not have the information, Ritchie would contact the leader of the team that dealt with the particular issue the Prime Minister was interested in.

You will find it as strange as I did when I discovered the Prime Minister was contacting Germain Denis directly and by-passing the Minister for International Trade, Pat Carney, Simon Reisman and Gordon Ritchie.

The Prime Minister was in direct contact with Germain Denis at least twice a week. I am certain that the reader, at this point, must be asking the question, how does she know this? The answer is quite simple really, as Germain Denis told me himself. He was always notified in advance by one of the Prime Minister's aides that the P.M. would be calling in, but there were times when they did not have a specific time for the appointed telephone call. On those days, Denis would order me to stay at my desk during the lunch break, in case the Prime Minister called. I was told by Denis that if he was away from his desk when the call came through, I was to locate him immediately. Also noteworthy is the fact that the only time Germain Denis ever closed the door to his office was when he was having a conversation with Mulroney.

This whole scenario raised a lot of red flags for me as I was a long time federal public servant working for senior level officials. In all my thirty some years, I never saw this "Chain of Command" broken.

Chapter 5

"GEAC"

God's Electronic Answer to Computers
Or
Spook System?

The Roget's Thesaurus states: *the informal definition of the word* <u>spook</u> *is "A person who secretly observes others to obtain information".*

According to GEAC's Website : <u>www.exgeac.info/geactime.html</u>:

- ✓ One of the founders, Gus German, states that GEAC does not stand for anything.

- ✓ GEAC claims that the company started doing business with only $50.00 and two men: Bob Isserstedt and Gus German. In 1975, GEAC Canada Limited is created. GEAC claims that the name "Geac" was registered in the USA in October 1978, seven years after they incorporated in Canada.

Was it strictly owned by the Americans at the time of the Canada-USA Free Trade Negotiations in 1986?

GEAC was brought into the Canadian Trade Negotiations Office by Canadian, Peter Hines.

An investigation carried out by the Trade Negotiations Security Office reports that GEAC is American owned with an American citizen at the helm.

In September-October 1986, Canadian Security at the Free Trade Negotiations Office removes GEAC system.

The Ottawa Citizen, on its front page reports that a <u>1.2 Million $ Computer System</u> is removed from the Trade Negotiations Office.

The question is WHY?

The following is a detailed account of the events that took place behind the scenes. It will provide you with the answer and will also explain why this million dollar system was removed from the Trade Negotiations Office, under orders from Deputy Chief Negotiator, Gordon Ritchie.

The GEAC computer system was already in place when I arrived on the scene in July 1986. Since my job was mostly administrative, I had several secretaries who worked for the officials who reported to Germain Denis and hence were the ones to input all documents prepared for the negotiations onto their computers. Each one of them had a "secret" password to access entry into their computers and the files. As the material also involved Memoranda to Federal Cabinet Ministers and the Prime Minister, the level of security involved was labeled "Top Secret" and no one but these secretaries and their bosses knew their password.

Late on a Friday evening, when everyone had gone home, I received a phone call from the Executive Assistant to the Deputy Minister of Multilateral Trade, a Mrs. Sylvia Ostry (Bernard Ostry's wife). Reportedly, Mrs. Ostry was taking a flight to the U.S. that night and needed a particular document that was on the computer of one of the secretaries. I explained to the E.A. that unless Peter Hines, the Head of our Computer Unit, was still at the office, it would be impossible for me to access the document since I did not have any of the passwords.

I also told her that I would seek out Hines and call her back. As luck would have it, Hines was in his office. After telling him what was needed, I asked him if he had the passwords for everyone at the Trade Negotiations Office. Hines replied NO he did not, but that the **President of GEAC had a "God Password".**

My immediate response was: "the God Password" what the heck is that?" Hines then proceeded to explain to me that this was a password that only the President of GEAC had in his possession. I thought that this meant that the President of GEAC could access the main frame serving the TNO computers. What a shock it was when Hines added that the President of GEAC had direct access to every computer in the Trade Negotiations Office, including Reisman's.

To verify if this was indeed true, instead of making an issue over the breach of security, I only asked Hines to immediately contact the President of GEAC so that we could obtain the document urgently needed by Mrs. Ostry. Approximately ten minutes later, Peter appeared at my desk with the requested document.

I then knew with certainty that all Memoranda to Cabinet, all negotiating strategies and all information used in the negotiations were all compromised. In fact, all Top Secret Memoranda to the Prime Minister's Office and to the Privy Council Office were all at risk.

Since this incident had taken place on a Friday evening, I could not take any action with TNO's Head of Security until the Monday morning. At approximately 8:00 a.m. on the Monday morning, I arrived at the Trade Negotiations Office and went straight into the Head of Security's office. Guy Marcoux was rather surprised to see me walking into his office without an appointment, so he knew that something was up.

I explained to Marcoux the discovery that I had made on the Friday night. I was appalled at Marcoux's reaction. He asked me point blank "Why are you bringing this matter to my attention?" He saw nothing wrong with it. It had to be explained to him that there was the possibility of GEAC being an American owned company and that since the President had this "God" password to access all of the negotiating documents, that perhaps this GEAC company was just a front and that it's President could be an American. If he was, this meant that he was in a position to provide the American team with all of our classified strategies, working papers, Top Secret Memoranda to Cabinet, etc. This would definitely be a huge advantage for the American team. After arguing the matter for almost two hours, I was unable to convince Marcoux to investigate GEAC's background. Why was Marcoux being so irresponsible? As Head of TNO's Security he should have jumped all over this and instantly seen the merit of my complaint.

I was not going to give up. I marched out of Marcoux's office and went straight to Gordon Ritchie's Office. I knew from experience that Ritchie respected and carefully listened to what any member of his staff had to say and he had the power and the authority to force Marcoux to investigate.

Unlike Marcoux, Ritchie took what I told him very seriously. He immediately ordered Marcoux to carry out a full investigation on GEAC. Approximately 48 hours later, the investigator reported back to Ritchie that the Americans were behind the GEAC Corporation.

Ritchie then came to me and advised me that GEAC Representatives would be coming to Ottawa the very next day to meet with me. He generously offered the use of his office for my meeting. He felt that not only would it give us some privacy, but would also empower me to deal with the GEAC Reps on a level playing field.

The next morning, three representatives from GEAC arrived at the Trade Negotiations Office at the appointed time. As pre-arranged with Gordon Ritchie, we met in his office. The meeting lasted for more than two (2) hours. During the entire meeting I said nothing and just listened to what they had to say. Their communication skills were strictly restricted to high tech jargon. At the end, as a gesture of power and authority, I moved my chair back and stood up while all three GEAC Reps remained seated. All I said was: "Gentlemen, with all the technical gibberish that I have listened to for the past two hours, I am left with only one question. If someone sets up an office across the street from the Trade Negotiations Office, can they have access to the data in all 110 TNO computers?" The answer was "YES" they can. "Well! Gentlemen, what you have just told me is that your GEAC system is NOT SECURE and with that kind of answer there is only one decision that I can make and that is the system has to go."

As reported in the Ottawa Citizen, that following weekend, the GEAC system was removed from the TNO as per Gordon Ritchie's orders.

What I do not know to this day, is why Peter Hines, who knew that this GEAC system was totally insecure, was allowed to bring it into the Trade Negotiations Office. Hines knew that GEAC was American owned and he also knew how important it was to the Prime Minister that Canada signed an Agreement with the U.S. How could we reach a fair and just agreement for Canada if the Americans could spy on us?

Hines also knew that highly sensitive material that would be classified "Top Secret" would be put onto the GEAC system. GEAC would have also been aware that Top Secret Memoranda to Cabinet with the Canadian Team's strategies would be on these computers.

Surely, Hines knew that the President of any non-governmental organization should not have access to any Canadian classified documents. Who gave Peter Hines the contract to bring in GEAC? And why was he allowed to keep his job at the Trade Negotiations Office after the discovery of the GEAC security breach, the very company that he was responsible for bringing into the negotiations?

Strangely enough, Germain Denis, who claimed to hate computers and refused to have one installed in his own office, was the one who met with Peter Hines on many occasions in his office behind a closed door. Was Denis in on this conspiracy? Perhaps this was the reason why he was so furious with me to the point of being insulting when he found out that I was the person responsible for not only discovering the security breach, but for having this multi-million dollar system removed from the TNO. Denis actually shouted at me in front of several co-workers, "Who the hell do you think you are? Someone at your level should not be handling such matters. Don't you ever handle anything again outside this office. Do you hear me?"

What I have found to be most intriguing is the fact that Peter Hines appeared on the cover page of several Canadian and non-Canadian magazines a few years after the Trade Negotiations Office closed its doors. Why the sudden popularity and stardom? Hines had become the latest Canadian millionaire.

N.B. Confirmation that the author was responsible for the above-noted event is evidenced by the Performance Review and Employee Appraisal report signed by Assistant Chief Negotiator, Germain Denis. {See Appendix "B"—page 2}

Chapter 6

The Briefing Books

Canadians were told that even though the U.S. and Canada did not require the signatures of our provincial premiers on the final text of the Free Trade Agreement, the Premiers would be kept apprised of what was being negotiated. The Premiers were told that this would be done through briefings that would take place after each negotiating session.

What the Premiers were not told was that prior to their briefing sessions, the documents used at the negotiating table would be altered. They would never see what had been truly given away. Hence began the trek along the path of deceit that would lead to the Americanization of Canada.

I did not know, until it was too late, the part that I would be playing in this staged theatrics of deceit and betrayal. It all began at midnight after the Canadian Team had returned from their first negotiating session in Washington. At approximately 10:00 p.m., I had gone home believing that my work was done for the day. In my head I was already prioritizing my work load for the next morning. I knew it would involve the preparation of the briefing books that had to be ready for the premiers with whom the team was meeting with the next morning. Imagine my surprise when Germain Denis contacted me at home around 11:00 p.m. and ordered me to return to the Trade Negotiations Office immediately and ordered me not to even tell my husband where I was going.

Another shock was still to come. Denis, like a spy in the night, then informed me that I had to avoid the Commissionaire {Security Guard} at the Reception Desk because he did not want us to have to sign in. Denis also stated that it was of vital importance that no one must ever know that we had come in to work in the middle of the night. "No one must know" he said. At this point, I did not understand why. But I was soon to find out.

I was told to meet him at a particular elevator in the garage because he had a key that would allow us in and bypass all security. When we finally arrived at my office, he ordered me to sit down at my computer and pull up the file on Subsidies. He then told me to create a second file on "Subsidies" and add the words "Provincial file". Denis then told me to type in the numbers he would provide and delete the paragraphs that he would identify. Denis went on to say "after we finish with the Subsidies issue, you will print out one copy of the one where we altered the figures and deleted the paragraphs. That's the copy that will be given to the provinces. Once you have the provincial file printed out, you will delete it from the system; by that I mean you do not just delete it from your hard drive, but you also delete it from the hard drive of the main frame located in the main computer centre. That way no one can trace it."

"We will repeat this process until we have gone through every topic that I am responsible for: i.e. subsidies, intellectual property, agriculture, energy, water, pharmaceuticals, etc etc., until every subject has its own "provincial file". Once you are done, you will take the original briefing books that were actually used in Washington and you will lock them up in my safe that's in my office—not yours—your area is too open to everyone—we have to make sure that there is no possibility of prying eyes."

The next step I was told was to number the "provincial" briefings books from 1 to 10 and to keep a list of which province had which number. Denis explained that this was a precautionary measure, in case someone decided to walk off with his or her book. This procedure would allow us to quickly track down which provincial representative had left with their Briefing Book and we would be able to immediately retrieve it. Denis said that it was crucial that the provincial reps not be given the opportunity to have the time to have a close look at the contents. Denis further stated that for that very reason, the briefing books could never be given out to the provincial reps until the last second and not until they were in the meeting room, and for that same reason I had to retrieve them the minute the briefing was over.

After that first briefing session, Germain Denis then instructed me to destroy nine of the briefing books and only keep one in a file in his safe. This had to be done after each negotiating session in order for Denis to be able to verify and keep track of what he had altered and deleted. This altered provincial version would tell him whether to raise or lower the figures last used. This process would have to be repeated after each negotiating session.

The premiers gracefully accepted the delay in receiving their briefing books for the first two briefing sessions. But, after that 2nd briefing, they were so upset that they contacted the Prime Minister's Office to express their discontent and demanded that the PMO resolve this unacceptable situation. They needed the Briefing Books to be given to them with sufficient lead time, prior to their briefing sessions with the Feds, in order to provide them with the opportunity to review the contents and to also be given the chance to bring forth their areas of concern as well as resolutions that could be brought to the negotiating table. The Premiers were never given the opportunity to have significant input. What did the PMO do? What everyone else does in government pass the buck on to the Privy Council Office (PCO).

Throughout the entire negotiations, PCO's Harry Swain had to contact me and demand that the briefing books be handed to the premiers ahead of time. Harry, for awhile, thought that the delay was my fault. I had to let him believe this because Germain Denis was not going to admit that he was under orders by the Prime Minister to never allow this to happen.

When Harry Swain was unsuccessful in his quest for the premiers to get their briefing books with sufficient lead time, the premiers went to the mainstream media. Still, nothing was done about it. We continued to give out the briefing books at the last minute once the premiers were in the meeting room. No one could understand how come Germain Denis could get away with defying the Privy Council Office. But I knew and couldn't tell.

To this day, I will always wonder what would have happened to this country if the premiers had known the truth at the time of these events. Would our premiers have stood up for the good of our country and its citizens? I am sorry to have to tell my readers that the answer is NO. In 1993, when my lawyer assisted me in exposing the wrongdoings that went on in the Trade Negotiations Office, he took it upon himself to notify all premiers. (A copy of his letter is at Appendix D). The Premiers did nothing. As you are surely aware, Canada and its citizens are in difficult economic times. Unemployment is high and the few jobs that are out there are being given away to foreigners. Small businesses are being shut down, etc. etc.

The plans developed by those in power are making progress in leaps and bounds towards a society that will only consist of KINGS and SERFS. Maude Barlow, National Chairperson, Council of Canadians, and Bruce Campbell, Research Fellow at the Canadian Centre for Policy Alternatives said it best when they made the following statements in their book, TAKE BACK THE NATION: "What we offer is a blueprint for survival . . . . If the powers in government cannot save our nation, the Canadian people must."

" . . . . Canadians have been too complacent. We have taken democracy for granted and have not accepted personal responsibility for its survival. Sleepwalking towards extinction, we have surrendered the decisions on our political lives to self-interested elites." "Our history has been one of trust in authority, and that authority has betrayed us."

Chapter 7

The Christmas Offering

www.time-is-fun.com

"WICKED SANTA CLAUSE"

Chapter 7

The Christmas Offering

(December 1986)

What happened that day came as a shock to me. I did not know how far a man in Germain Denis' position was willing to go. A few days prior to Christmas, when all the support staff was being taken out for Christmas luncheons, Mr. Denis asked me to meet him at the Delta Hotel located at 350 Sparks Street in Ottawa for a Christmas lunch. I was quite surprised at this offer as he was not known for his generosity towards staff and in the spirit of Christmas I accepted. As a matter of fact, he was so cheap, that at one point when he went on a business trip to Brussels, it was his wife who brought me back a box of chocolates.

When I arrived at the Delta, he was already waiting for me in the lounge and told me to follow him. I thought I was being brought to a private dining room and truly believed that he had booked it to have the opportunity to buy lunch for his loyal and hardworking staff. When he opened the door I was shocked to find myself in one of Delta's bedroom suites. When he saw the look of shock on my face and went several paces ahead of me, turned around to face me and said "Shelley Ann, I thought I would offer myself as your Christmas present instead of buying you a gift".

It took me all of two seconds to take in the scene as he stood there already stripping his clothes off. I left the room extremely upset as I knew that my refusal would cause me problems later. Despite my haste to leave the Delta Hotel, I fortunately had the presence of mind to go up to the front desk and ask for a copy of the bill for the room. I explained to the clerk on duty that I was Germain Denis' Executive Assistant and as such was responsible for handling all his monetary expenditures. The Clerk handed me the invoice and the receipt for the room. It had already been paid for in cash and was in the name of G.A. Denis, but he had used a Montreal address.

Unfortunately, even though I refused to accommodate Denis's needs he continued to demand sexual favours throughout the two years of the negotiations. It did not matter to him that I kept refusing him and he could not even see beyond his needs that he was actually guilty of sexual harassment.

For two years Denis put me through hell. Everytime I refused him, he shouted insults at me in front of my colleagues. One day, after I had refused to go and meet him in a Montreal Hotel while he was on business, he went as far as calling me stupid, that I must be on drugs and could not do my job. I was doing everything wrong. If this was true, why did my attempts to get transferred out of his office fail?

I do not recollect how many times I approached the Human Resources personnel at the headquarters office of Foreign Affairs to transfer me out of Denis' office, but according to the personnel officers, Denis had already ordered them not to remove me from his office under any circumstances and they were so afraid of him that they obeyed his orders.

One honest personnel officer, exposed the extent to which Denis was prepared to go to when he told her that I could only be removed over his dead body. She said they were all told that they were not to reassign me under any circumstances.

After this latest exposé, I was more determined than ever to get myself out of his office. I made the decision to approach Gordon Ritchie, whom I knew to be a very fair person.

I did not want to cause any hassles at this point and therefore did not tell Ritchie about the sexual harassment that I had to endure over the past two years. I just told him that for personal reasons it was imperative that I find a job elsewhere and asked if he could help me.

He told me he would only be too happy to oblige and to go back to my desk and he would be in touch with me. Shortly, after, Mr. Ritchie gave me a copy of a letter that he had written to the Head of the International Monetary Fund in Washington, Mr. Marcel Masse, former Under Secretary of State for Foreign Affairs.

As a result, Mr. Massé responded to me personally and he let me know how happy he would be to have me at IMF, but I still had to go through their Human Resources Office. Unfortunately, when I received their letter, the offer was for a junior position and being a single mom with two teenage boys to look after, the salary would not have been sufficient to support us in Washington. I felt I had no choice, but to decline.

Women in the Proverbial Political Arena

What is the "proverbial political arena"? It is not necessarily a politician's office. It can be the OFFICE of any high ranking individual in the private sector; in any government office, agency or any non-governmental organization.

Any woman who has worked in this arena knows the "unspoken" rule. If you are a woman and you want to jump start your career, you have sex with the right man. Who is this right man? He is the one who holds a position as a senior executive. He is the one who behaves and believes that he is God. He is the one who has the power to create and destroy a human being in one breath. He puts you on a high pedestal one minute and then, in that one crucial moment when you refuse his sexual advances without remorse or a single thought to your welfare, he immediately proceeds to destroy you and your career.

I have experienced this scenario many times in my career, and that is why I never made it into management. Why did I refuse? Because I would not allow my moral values and my integrity to be compromised. I firmly believe that the behavior of these officials is criminal in nature. How can the "proverbial system" give them that kind of power over any human being? To destroy a human being because she would not have sex with an individual should be punishable by law.

You have a Union that you can present your grievance to, but in the end, the Union folds under the political pressures. All of a sudden, a strong case is undermined and weakened. All of a sudden, there is an offer on the table to settle out of the Hearing Room. The offer is not the position that was sought because the person qualified, but a mere pittance of a substitution.

The position you sought is given to "Belinda Bloe" who is more than willing to sleep her way to the top. Never mind that this talent is her only qualification for the job. It does not matter to "Joe What's-his-name" that this person cannot do the job and that this fact alone affects every employee in his kingdom. Everyone has to do overtime to make up for this one person's deficiency. "Joe What's-his-name" forgets that this person's inability to do the job also affects everyone, from the public in general, to his colleagues.

YET, females who are federal public servants either say YES or they lose everything. Why? because it is a Just-Us system that we have in this country. The unions, the human rights tribunals and the federal courts crumble under the pressures of politics.

Chapter 8

Under the Veil of Secrecy
The Shredding at Midnight

NINE PROVINCIAL BRIEFING BOOKS HAD TO DISAPPEAR. Denis had to destroy the evidence so he ordered me to shred them in the middle of the night. Each time he only kept one copy. Why? Because he had to know where he was at with the altered figures and deleted chapters. Denis had to keep track because if he didn't he would have made mistakes that would have been obvious and he would have been caught in the act.

In Chapter 6, I dealt with the issue of the provincial premiers being duped into believing that they were being provided with the actual briefing books that had been used in Washington.

When Germain Denis ordered me to create a "dummy" briefing book for the provinces, we had to create a second file on the computer that we named "the provincial file". This is the file that we used to alter figures and delete chapters. Since this activity was highly unorthodox and filled with deceit, it became a "top secret" project. Not only were the provincial reps deceived, so was the whole country.

As you will see from the List of Meetings between Germain Denis and the provinces attached at Appendix "C", the activities described above took place over the period of one year; i.e. from January 18, 1987 to January 26, 1988.

Prior to each meeting, the "top secret" midnight process took place. Each time, I would have to create, alter and then delete the "fake" provincial file. I would then have to produce 10 copies for ten briefing books.

After each briefing session, I had to again go into the Trade Negotiations Office at midnight and by-pass security. This time it was to secretly shred nine of the ten provincial briefing books. Denis always had to keep one as this was crucial for him to know where he was at with the altered figures. If he had previously shown that Canada had negotiated agriculture at 50% and the premiers felt this was too much then Denis would have to bring down the figure to 40% the next time he showed them the fake briefing books. This activity took place for every issue that Denis was responsible for. These issues were Subsidies, Agriculture, Energy, Water, Intellectual Property, Pharmaceuticals, Health Care and Lumber.

The most significant issue was the giving away of our water. I was ordered by Germain Denis to delete the entire chapter dealing with OUR water. Not only were Canadians being deceived, but our most precious resource was being given away without a second thought as what this would do to Canadians in the future. Denis knew that the provinces could never find out the truth and therefore proceeded to order me to delete the chapter on water for every provincial briefing book. This deceit was taking place at the same time that Maude Barlow was voicing her sharp opposition to the FTA on Parliament Hill because she believed Canadians were being lied to when they were told that WATER was not on the negotiating table. Barlow was right. YES, WATER WAS ON THE TABLE but only the Federal Government negotiating team knew. All the provinces, as well as the Canadian public, were lied to.

I will take this opportunity to expand on the subject of WATER as it is the most precious commodity for every country in the world.

A study prepared in the U.S. for Greenpeace has renewed the debate over who has access to Canada's water. In the documents that I saw it states: "contained water" in the U.S.-Canada free-trade agreement can mean water behind a dam. In their cover-up, the negotiators used the words self-contained in order to mislead Canadians to mean bottled water.

The distinction would enable the GRAND canal—a $100 billion water diversion project to the U.S. from James Bay to proceed, according to secret documents that I saw as one of the FTA's proof readers. This GRAND CANAL would pave the way to reroute massive amounts of water to the U.S.

According to a research done in 1990, a project on the shores of Ontario's and Quebec's James Bay promises to bring it all home to U.S. consumers.

At the end of this chapter I have included a map that I discovered on the internet depicting the proposed plans that would lead to a huge sacrifice for this northern area and for all Canadians.

The Canada-U.S. Free Trade Agreement (FTA) and the North American Free Trade Agreement (NAFTA) essentially prevent Canada and any of its provinces from placing restrictions on the export of water.

Dave Marshall of the Department of International Trade in Ottawa said the report misrepresents bottled water as contained water behind a dam.

Researchers on this issue have reported that water impounded behind a dam is not free-flowing and would therefore be considered an economic good under the FTA and NAFTA. These free trade deals could force Canada to "turn on the tap".

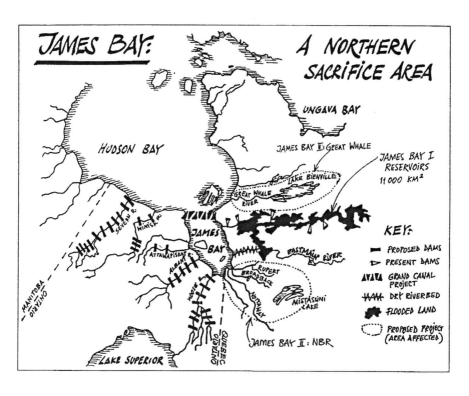

"MAP OF JAMES BAY"

Chapter 9

Who Wanted the Deal the Most?

Was there reciprocity? NO there wasn't. It was a WIN-WIN situation only for the Americans. The negotiations did not go well for Canada. WHY?

It was apparent to everyone right from the beginning that Canada was desperate for this deal, not the U.S. It was the Canadian experts who advised the Prime Minister that a free trade deal with the U.S. would indeed bode very well for Canada. It took a lot of persuasion from the Canadian side to convince the Americans to enter into negotiations.

Hospitality American style vs Canadian

A prominent example was how our Canadian Team was treated went they went to Washington in comparison to the way Canada treated the American Team that came to Ottawa. When the American Team came to Ottawa we took care of all their travel arrangements from their accommodation in Ottawa's better hotels to the hiring of a shuttle bus with a chauffeur to transport the American Team from the airport to their hotel and then from their hotel to the Trade Negotiations Office. Canada hosted, served and picked up the tab for their breakfasts, lunches and dinners while they were in town. The Americans were treated like royalty.

Now! On the other hand, when our Canadians went to Washington, we had to make their travel and hotel arrangements and the team had to find a taxi cab from the airport to bring them to the USTR building in downtown Washington. They had to make their own arrangements to travel between the USTR building and their hotel. One member of the team reported that they were so busy they had no time to go out for lunch so they either did without or one of the Canadian team members had to go out and bring back sandwiches. The Americans never reciprocated. The Americans did not even offer the Canadian Team a sandwich.

There is one incident that I remember quite vividly. This particular incident occurred because I had been told that the Canadian Team was only going to Washington for one day; therefore no overnight accommodations were required. But, by 8 o'clock in the evening, it became evident that the team would have to stay overnight. Did the Americans assist our team and arrange for overnight accommodation? NO they did not. Instead, one of our negotiators had to call Reisman's Executive Assistant and myself in Ottawa to ask us to return to the Free Trade Office in order to make calls to Washington and try to find them hotel rooms; cancel and reschedule all flight reservations, etc. We were at the office until 4:00 a.m. and I had to come back by 8:00 a.m. the next morning. Do not tell me or anyone else that the Americans could not have been more courteous and reciprocated by making a few phone calls. And, the Canadian public is told on a daily basis that they are "our" friends.

How unimportant the deal was for the Americans was in evidence everywhere. Canada's Globe and Mail newspaper kept producing cartoons that clearly demonstrated that Canada, in their desperation to cut a deal, was giving away our country. This was clearly depicted in one particular cartoon where Peter Murphy is standing at the top of a very long table filled to the brim with Canadian goodies, while Simon Reisman stood in front of a very short table with nothing on it. That one cartoon not only said it all, but it told the truth, unfortunately I was unable to locate this particular cartoon.

Was this a good deal for Canada? Has Joe Bloe, Canadian citizen, seen the whole Free Trade Deal? Twenty-four years later Canadians only know what the events have shown since 1988. If that is not enough to convince them that Canada got the short end of the stick I don't know what will convince them to stand up and take back their country.

Chapter 10

Historical Weekend
The Hours Before Midnight

Where is President Reagan?

THE REAGAN RESIDENCE

Chapter 10

Historical Weekend

Simon Reisman, his Canadian Negotiating Team and Derek Burney, Chief of Staff to the Prime Minister, returned to the negotiating table in Washington on October 2nd, 1987, after Reisman had walked out on the talks on September 2nd.

The following is a chronology of what went on behind the scenes during those long hours before the "MIDNIGHT" deadline of October 3rd.

On October 1, 1987

At approximately 10:30 p.m. Simon Reisman's Executive Assistant and I were contacted at home and were ordered to immediately return to the Trade Negotiations Office to deal with the travel arrangements for the entire Canadian negotiating team of 35 officials.

At 11:00 p.m, I arrived at the Trade Negotiations Office only to discover that the impasse was still on. I was asked to remain on stand-by.

At 11:40 p.m, Germain Denis contacted me to report that Mulroney had spoken to Reisman at approximately 11:30 p.m. The "impasse" had ended. Reportedly, the Prime Minister ordered Reisman back to Washington on the very first flight leaving Ottawa the next morning.

October 2, 1987

At around midnight, I received a phone call from an official from the Department of National Defense (DND) who confirmed that authorization for the use of the Challenger aircraft had been given, but due to seating restrictions, several flights would be needed to accommodate all 35 officials of the Canadian Team. Since they all had to arrive at the U.S. Trade Representatives building in Washington at the same time since this is where the working groups for both sides would be hammering out the FTA deal, it was decided that it would not be feasible to use the Challenger for all 35 officials. The decision was made between the DND official and I that only the senior negotiators from the Trade Negotiations Office would travel with the Challenger and the rest of the team would travel by commercial airline. This agreed upon, Reisman's Executive Assistant and I remained at the Trade Negotiations Office until 4:00 a.m. on October 2nd to finalize all arrangements.

The following is an account of the historical weekend as reported to me by Germain Denis who was in touch with me by phone throughout the entire time the Canadian Team was in Washington. By mid-morning, the Canadian Team arrived in Washington. Several hours after arriving at the U.S. Trade Representative's offices, Simon Reisman discovered, to his dismay, that the real action was taking place in the Treasury Building, two blocks away in James Baker's Star Chamber. Reisman had not been invited to be party to the "star" team. Reportedly, the two teams worked through the day and throughout the night to arrive at a palatable agreement for both sides.

October 3, 1987

The hours before the "midnight" deadline of October 3rd seemed like an eternity for the Canadian Team. By 10:00 p.m. on the night of October 3rd, the Prime Minister's Office kept calling and ordering that we try and contact President Ronald Reagan to find out where the negotiations stood. Time was running out. The deadline was at midnight and no one could reach the President and no word was coming out of James Baker's Star Chamber. At approximately 11:00 p.m, I was asked to at least contact Reagan's top aide and try to get some information as to where the President was.

To my dismay, I received confirmation of how unimportant these negotiations were to the U.S. and its President. When I finally reached Reagan's top aide, I was informed that: *"the President could not be disturbed as he was watching a rerun of one of his movies."* Reportedly, the President was watching a rerun of his movie, "BEDTIME FOR BONZO". And the clock kept ticking away getting closer and closer to midnight and still no word from the President or from the Star Chamber. One member of the Canadian Team told me that Reisman was not only furious at being kept outside the loop, but was also seriously agitated.

Reportedly, at precisely 3 minutes before midnight, the Canadian Team received a phone call from the Star Chamber. An OUTLINE of the deal had been signed. A deal that meant the death of our country. A deal that meant that our beloved Canada would be changed forever—better for the wealthy—but far worse for the middle class, middle income Canadian.

Chapter 11

Press Conference/Sneaking out the FTA

I saw this OUTLINE as I was the one who brought it to the Prime Minister the next day. What I found strange was that even though I was told that Reisman was not in the Star Chamber the evening of October 3rd, Reisman's signature appeared on the last page along with Michael Wilson's, Finance Minister, Pat Carney's, Federal Cabinet Minister for International Trade, Derek Burney's, Chief of Staff to the Prime Minister and of course from the U.S. Team, James Baker's, Clayton Yeutter's, McPherson's and Peter Murphy's. When and where was Reisman when he signed the Agreement.?

On the morning of October 4, 1987, the Canadian Negotiating Team returned to Ottawa. Germain Denis informed me that he had the signed deal with him. That really surprised me that Reisman did not have it as he was the Chief Negotiator and Leader of the Canadian Team. The buzz of excitement in the TNO was in evidence everywhere. Everyone was preparing to attend Reisman's Press Conference that was going to be held at the Conference Centre in downtown Ottawa for early afternoon.

By Noon, all negotiators had left the TNO. Shortly after their departure, I received a phone call from Mulroney's top aide, Bernard Roy. Roy told me that the Prime Minister wanted to table the Free Trade Agreement in the House of Commons at 2:00 p.m. that same day. Therefore, could I please do whatever was necessary to obtain the FTA Outline and bring it to the Prime Minister's Office asap. Roy also told me that it was important to get it out of the Conference Centre without the media discovering that I had it. The Prime Minister did not want the media to see it and if they knew I had it in my hands they would try to stop me and insist on seeing it. I told Roy, that Yes, I could achieve this task.

It was almost 1:00 p.m. and I had to reach the Conference Centre, find Germain Denis amongst a sea of journalists and television crews from all over the country. Remember that Germain Denis, for reasons I did not understand, was the one who had the signed Agreement Outline in his briefcase.

I quickly went to the Taxi stand at the front of the building and ordered the driver to take me to the Conference Centre as fast as he could. I explained that I was running an errand for the Prime Minister and I needed for him to wait for me at the door of the Conference Centre so that he could bring me straight to Mulroney's Office at the Centre Block of Parliament Hill. Time was of the essence as it was now past 1:00 p.m. and Mulroney wanted to table the Agreement at 2:00 p.m. and was waiting for me.

I made the mistake of telling the taxi cab driver to speed it up, that he was going too slow. Knowing that Mulroney would not be understanding if we did not make it to Parliament Hill on time, the driver sped through downtown Ottawa streets at speeds only reserved for the expressways in Europe. I became terrified when he started going through red lights and with speeds that would have frightened anyone, the driver totally disregarded the laws that govern our safety rules on Canadian roads. We finally arrived at the Conference Centre in minutes and with shaky knees I stumbled out of the cab and entered the building that was swarming with media people from wall to wall. I had to fight my way to the front where Reisman stood at the podium. Looking on was Denis and the other negotiators. I finally managed to get close enough to Denis to tug at his sleeve to get his attention. I then whispered my orders in his ear. I then told Denis to drop to the floor so no one could see what we were up to. Once we were both kneeling down on the floor, Denis opened his brief case and I opened mine.

Denis transferred the Agreement to my brief case and with one swift movement closed it. This seemingly insignificant act would change the Canada that we knew to the Canada that you and I know today. No one knew at the time to what extent all of our lives would change because of this final act.

Thank God! that I was an unknown entity to the media at that point in time. Fortunately, I had already been labeled an "unknown phantom entity", aka "de novo" by Simon Reisman in his CBC interview with the late Mister Canada broadcaster, Peter Gzowski. Thus, being transparent I was able to slither through the crowded room without being noticed and no one tried to stop me. Even Reisman and Ritchie did not know what had just happened. I jumped into the waiting cab and we sped off to Parliament Hill.

When I arrived at the House of Commons' Centre Block, I thought that I would have to go through the standard procedure of having to present my ID and that the Commissionaire would then contact Mulroney's Office and that someone would come down and get the document. NO, NOT THIS TIME. As soon as I identified myself, I was escorted to a waiting elevator and with no stops I was brought to the floor where the Prime Minister's Office was located. Before I reached the doors to enter the Reception Area of his office, I was greeted by Mulroney himself and his top aide, Bernard Roy. The minute I took the signed Agreement out of my briefcase, Mulroney snatched it out of my hands. I quickly reacted and snatched it away from Mulroney. I hastily explained that before he could have it, I wanted Roy and I to verify that all the pages were there. I certainly did not want to be blamed if there were any missing pages. I was shocked that Mulroney said nothing and just nodded his acceptance of the situation and motioned Roy to do as I asked.

There was no table in the corridor and I was not invited inside their offices so Roy and I had to kneel down on the floor and use a chair to count and lay out the pages of the signed Agreement. There were 38 pages and none were missing. I handed over the document to Mulroney and Canada was about to be changed forever.

Approximately 48 hours after the deal was signed and put in the Prime Minister's hands, I received a phone call from someone who claimed to be calling from our secret service agency. This person asked me the strangest question. "Shelley Ann do you remember if the signatures on the Free Trade Agreement, were in different colors of ink?" I responded with "Yes they were". The person thanked me and terminated the call.

It had been a long road for Canada. Finally, an idea that was strictly a vision in 1846, one hundred and forty-two years later was to finally become reality.

WAS THIS A GOOD DEAL FOR CANADA? Twenty four years later many Canadians know that it wasn't. Unfortunately, too many are still wearing blindfolds.

Chapter 12

The Covert Disappearance of FTA documents & The Implementation Scheme & Warnings

In March 1988, as preparations were underway to close the Trade Negotiations Office (TNO), a Memorandum addressed to Assistant Chief Negotiators and all Section Heads was circulated throughout the TNO. This Memorandum was requesting that all working papers, without exception, including the briefing books that had been used in the negotiations, were to be handed over to the Head of the TNO's Information/Research Centre in order for her to catalogue the material and hand it over to Archives Canada.

I immediately brought this memo to Germain Denis's attention. I entered his office and was told "shut the door behind you and sit down." I was then informed that I had to help him out with something that was extremely sensitive and that had to be handled with absolute secrecy. When I looked at him with an extremely puzzled look on my face, he stated, "Let me clarify things for you". Denis then proceeded to explain that it was absolutely vital to immediately remove from the Trade Negotiations Office all of his Briefing Books and Working Files pertaining to the negotiations. Denis then ordered me to transport all documents to the trunk of his car. At this point he threw his car keys at me across the round table. He then repeated the words "with absolute secrecy—No one must know that you are doing this". He then proceeded to instruct me on 'How and When' since all the material was in his safe.

Denis then ordered me to listen very carefully to what he had to say, because if I didn't he would personally see to it that I would lose my job.

The instructions that Denis gave me were as follows: some are "direct quotes"; {others are the approximate wording that was used by Denis}

a.) "it has to be done very quickly—before the end of the day";

b.) "You're to put the material in Xerox paper boxes";

c.) {Then I want you to remove the material from the cabinet just a few pieces at a time—I want it to appear as if you're doing a cleaning out of the over packed files so as not to arouse suspicion};

d.) {I figure there should be approximately 7 boxes total—you must bring them down to my car one at a time at approximately two-hour intervals; one hour when you can. Tighten things up during the lunch break—there will be less people around.

e.) {And you pay attention to this last point or you will find yourself without a job.} "If anybody, at anytime, asks you any questions as to why I haven't handed over the material, you tell them that prior to the Memo being circulated, you had begun preparations for the shut down of this office and realizing the sensitivity of the material, you sent it all to Classified Waste to be shredded".

Germain Denis completely ignored the written orders outlined in the Memo that had been signed by Gordon Ritchie and Simon Reisman. The Memo stated: "that no one was to destroy any papers used in the negotiations unless they obtained prior approval from either Ritchie or Reisman".

I left his office, waited for half an hour and then proceeded with the assigned task. It was on my second trip down to Denis' car that there was a close encounter of the perpetrated theft being uncovered. I had just gotten on the elevator carrying a huge Xerox box when Phillip Tessier, Reisman's chauffeur jumped onto the elevator at the last second, just before the doors closed. Phillip, being the gentleman that he was, immediately offered to carry my box for me; when I refused, he insisted. In order not to arouse any suspicion, I let him take the box. Phillip then jokingly said, "God, Shelley Ann what in the heck is in the box? It's so heavy one could think that you were sneaking out gold bricks." I replied, "It's my huge Random House Dictionary that I'm taking back home".

I knew that there were two things that Phillip could not find out. One was what was in the box and second, where I was taking the box. I certainly could not tell him what was inside and I could not tell him that it was going to Denis' car or my own car. As the elevator speedily kept going downwards, I quickly had to come up with an answer that would ensure that I sent Phillip away without any knowledge of what was going on. I came to the realization that if there was ever an investigation as to the disappearance of these documents, I did not want Phillip to be able to swear in a court of law that he had taken these books to the trunk of my car.

When we reached the ground floor of 50 O'Connor Street, Phillip insisted that he take the box to my car. I had no choice but to bring him to it where it was located in the basement parking area. It occurred to me on the way that the only solution to my dilemma was to pretend that I had forgotten to bring my car keys. I knew that there was no way that I could let Phillip put that box inside the trunk. Therefore, when we arrived at our destination, I played the role of the "air head blonde" and said: "OH! Phillip, stupid me, I am so tired I forgot my car keys back in my office." Phillip then offered to stay at the car with the Xerox box while I went back to get my car keys. I thought OH My God, how do I get rid of this guy. As he was Reisman's chauffeur, I figured that the most effective way to get rid of him was to impress upon him the fact that Reisman could need him at any moment and therefore he should go straight back to his office. Before he left, I asked him to hide the box under the front of the car. It was very important for me that Philippe not put the box inside my car. When he agreed to do so it was with a sigh of relief that I proceeded with the task at hand.

In 1993, when questioned by reporters about this incident, Phillip Tessier told all reporters that he had no recollection of this event.

After the incident with Reisman's chauffeur, I went back to my office only to fully realize the danger I was in for complying with Denis' orders. It was at this point that I fully comprehended the situation Denis had implicated me in. Badly shaken and frightened, I went in to his office and shut the door. I told him: "I don't want to continue with this—you had better do it yourself. I don't want to be party to any of this". This is when he threatened my entire career with the Federal Government.

<u>The Merger of Canada</u>
<u>With the</u>
<u>United States of America</u>

When I returned to my office, I proceeded with the task of screening the material that was to be taken away to Denis' car. While doing this task, I came across a document titled "Implementation Scheme". This document was drawn up as a chart and it depicted the steps that had to be taken and the events that had to occur before the Americans would agree to a merger with Canada. I was tempted to make a copy to prove to Canadians that we were being sold out, but as I have repeatedly informed Canadians on my guest speaking tours, I knew that if I did this, I would be arrested and would never have been able to bring the information to the Canadian public. As many of you already know, even though some of the conditions imposed by the U.S. have not occurred, we have, in fact, secretly merged with the U.S.

As further evidence of what I witnessed are articles that appeared on the front page of the Ottawa Citizen. At that time a book titled FROM HEARTLAND TO NORTH AMERICAN REGION STATE, penned by a Queens University Professor, appeared among dozens of similar writings. On January 28, 1998, a front page article of the Ottawa Citizen was titled "Ontario Ripe for Separatism". A day later, same source, front page, "Ontario Could Become Nation in itself". Again, a day later "National Ties Unraveling, (Premier) Harris Admits". The following day, front page, "Ontario Clearer Politically". On the fifth day "Ontario a Leader of Powerful New States". The "Implementation Scheme", as viewed by me, is in accordance with these publications and within this really much broader, suppressed context.

I returned to my office to continue the job of sifting through the working papers used in the negotiations so that I could identify the ones he wanted taken to the trunk of his car. As I was reading sections of the material, my attention was drawn to the document dealing with our Social Security Programs (Health Care, Old Age Security Pensions, Welfare, etc.). It was no wonder that Denis did not want these documents to reach Archives Canada. The material confirmed what John Turner and Maude Barlow had been voicing publicly. They were both accusing the Canadian government of harmonizing our Health Care system and Old Age Security pension with the U.S. Yet, the Canadian government kept insisting that these issues were not on the negotiating table.

Of course, there was no *"Whistle Blowing Act"* to protect federal public servants at the time and to this day we are still in this same situation. We are still fighting to get this Act passed. At Chapter 17, you will find the historical background on this Act.

The following are REPLICAS of two articles written by journalist, Alex Roslin, formerly of the Montreal Mirror.

September 16, 1993

FREE TRADE CHARADE

NEW EVIDENCE IN CLARK CASE

NEW EVIDENCE has emerged to support a federal employee's allegation of document tampering in the Canada-U.S. free trade talks.

Shelley Ann Clark, a 32-year veteran of the civil service, told the Mirror in August that her boss, top trade negotiator Germain Denis, ordered her to alter and shred documents to conceal what Ottawa gave away in the trade talks. Clark claimed Denis ordered her to destroy key documents that were used to brief the provinces about the status of the trade discussions.

Federal officials told the Mirror last month all trade-related documents were passed on to the National Archives after the trade talks were finished in 1987. But a government inventory has no listing for the documents Clark claims were destroyed. She claims this proves she is telling the truth. "It's the smoking gun".

The inventory does list papers related to "liaison with federal and provincial government agencies." But both Clark and Simon Reisman, Canada's ambassador to the trade talks, said last week this almost certainly refers to the papers of Alan Nymark, the trade office's liaison officer. Denis' papers would not be listed under "liaison," Clark and Reisman both said.

Clark has been on paid leave since December. During the trade talks, she was Denis' executive secretary. Denis, currently assistant deputy minister of multilateral commercial trade, did not return repeated calls but a spokesman said the trade department has no comment.

Free trade opponents have demanded an investigation of Clark's allegations. They argue that if the public had known what was given away in the trade talks, the Conservatives may not have been re-elected in 1988. But in a surprising reversal last week, the RCMP decided there was insufficient evidence to proceed with a police investigation. In mid-August, a Mountie spokesman said a formal inquiry would be launched by "early September."

Clark, who still has top-security clearance, sought access to the archives last week but she said she was told she could not see key government documents that would support her case. She added she was told that many of the papers still have not been handed over to the archives six years after the Free Trade Agreement was signed. These papers are in the custody of the Federal Records Office. Employees of this office did not return calls.

*   *   *

August 21, 1993

FREE TRADE CHARADE

INQUIRY SOUGHT ON FRAUD CLAIMS

FREE TRADE OPPONENTS are demanding an inquiry into allegations that this government used fraud to ram through the 1988 Canada-U.S. Free Trade Agreement.

Shelley Ann Clark, a veteran federal employee, told the Mirror last week that her boss, top trade negotiator Germain Denis, ordered her to alter and shred documents to conceal what Ottawa gave away in the trade talks.

"This should be fully and publicly investigated by the government and RCMP" said Maude Barlow, national chair of the Council of Canadians, an Ottawa-based group of free-trade opponents. "This is no nut we're talking about. We're talking about someone who had top security clearance."

If true, Barlow said the allegations mean Ottawa rammed through the Free Trade Agreement by defrauding Canadians. "This put the whole free trade process in jeopardy."

Clark is a 32-year veteran of the civil service who has been on paid leave since last December. During the trade talks, she was Denis' executive secretary. She has alleged in a sworn affidavit and in a statement to the RCMP that her boss repeatedly ordered her to alter briefing books used to keep the provinces informed about the trade talks. Clark also claimed she was ordered to shred classified papers to conceal document-tampering. An RCMP spokesman said the Mounties are looking into Clark's charges but have yet to launch an official investigation.

Denis, currently on vacation, is now assistant deputy minister of multilateral commercial trade. Trade department officials did not return repeated calls.

Tony Clarke, national chair of the Action Canada Network, a coalition of 50 groups opposing free trade, said if the provinces and the public had known what was given away, opposition to the trade agreement would have been stronger and the Conservatives may not have been re-elected in 1988.

At the time federal officials said regional development subsidies and other social programs were not discussed in trade talks. But Clarke said the new revelations suggest they probably were—something free trade opponents have long suspected.

Clarke cited the recent overhaul of the unemployment insurance system and cuts to federal transfer payments for medi care as examples of how many Canadian social programs are being brought in line with standards south of the border. U.S. health companies have long clamored for the right to bid for contracts from Canada's health system and since the FTA, firms have won that right, Clarke said.

*   *   *

Following a CTV (aka CJOH TV) broadcast, Canadians and Members of Parliament insisted that the RCMP investigate my allegations. Can you guess what action the RCMP took? YES! Like Ripley's Believe it or Not, they contacted Germain Denis by phone, and requested an appointment to go through his files. Denis, of course, agreed and set a date for approximately one week later. Do you wonder why they found nothing? (Refer to Chapter 23—Meeting with the RCMP in Jack Ramsay's office, Reform MP from Alberta).

The chart has been recreated from memory by the author. You will recall, earlier in this chapter, that I underlined the fact that I did not take a copy of the original scheme as I would have been arrested for stealing a top secret document. The Canadian Government and it's many agents never believed that I did not steal a copy and this led to the break-in and ransacking of my residence in Vienna, Austria and my Ottawa residence. Whenever I travelled for guest speaking engagements, my luggage never made it on board the aircrafts that I travelled on. Can you believe, that after we were airborne I would get a telegram apologizing for my luggage being too late to make it onto the aircraft I was travelling on but it would be delivered to me as a courtesy of the airline.

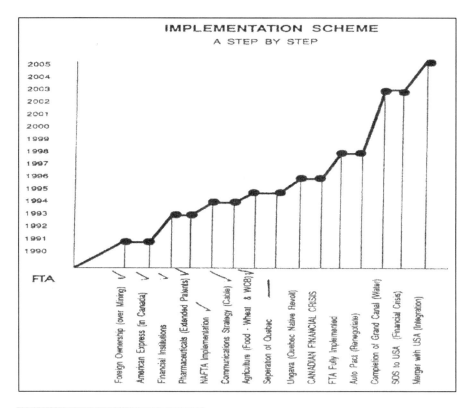

* For purposes of clarity the list has been retyped in larger font as follows:

- Foreign Ownership (over mining)   - 1990
- American Express in Canada   - 1991

- Financial Institutions — 1992
- Pharmaceuticals (Extended Patents) — 1993
- NAFTA Implementation — 1994
- Communications Strategy (Cable) — 1995
- Agriculture (Food, Wheat & WC8) — 1996
- Separation of Quebec — 1997
- Ungava (Quebec Native Revolt) — 1998
- CANADIAN FINANCIAL CRISIS — 1999
- FTA fully implemented — 2000
- Auto Pact (Renegotiate) — 2001
- Completion of Grand Canal (Water) — 2002
- SOS to U.S.A. (Financial Crisis) — 2003
- Merger with USA (Integration) — 2004-2005

Warnings reported in 1988 by the author / Were they Right or Wrong?

The following is a list of various areas that were affected by the signing of the Free Trade Agreement:

PROGRESSIVE OWNERSHIP OF CANADIAN RESOURCES AND FINANCIAL INSTITUTIONS

- AMEX BANK

  They used this bank to finance many of the changes. It was allowed into Canada by Mulroney.

- CANADIAN BANKS

  Paul Martin Jr. denies Canadian banks the right to become Canadian based major international banks. They have to grow offshore in order to weaken Canadian financial institutions.

- CANADIAN DOLLAR

  Is being maintained at levels that encourage foreign ownership of Canadian resources and companies.

EXTENSION OF PHARMACEUTICAL PATENT PROTECTION

- Passed in the House of Commons. This Increased the cost of drugs to all Canadians.

EROSION OF MEDICARE

- Continued under-funding to cause crises that will persude Canadians to accept privatization.

- The entry of American companies to provide hospitals and other health services to Canadians.

IMPLEMENTATION OF NAFTA

North American Free Trade Agreement. An Agreement between the U.S. and Mexico and Canada. NOT TO BE CONFUSED WITH THE FTA. That is the FREE TRADE AGREEMENT BETWEEN CANADA & THE U.S.

NAFTA was created and orchaestrated in order to confuse Canadians and to hide all that was being given away. With Canadians focusing on the FTA, the majority of Canadians did not bother to have a closer look at NAFTA and therefore did not object to it.

If Canadians had been given the opportunity to have a closer look at NAFTA they would have seen that it was:

- Completed with more benefits than anyone expected, BUT TAKE A LOOK AT THE PROVISIONS THAT: Allow private U.S. companies to sue the Canadian Government for damages caused by Public Policy decisions made for the benefit of Canadians.

INTEGRATION OF TELECOMMUNICATIONS

- ALL Canadian Media Institutions are being swamped by the U.S. media.

  THEIR PLAN: To manage the perception of Canadians in such a way as to ensure the acceptance of their plans without protest.

  A MOCKERY is being made of Canadians attempting to take control of their own lives, the future of their children and their living environment.

  THEIR GOAL: Eliminate the Middle Class and return US to a Society of Kings and Serfs.

SEPARATION OF QUEBEC

Those in power who had Lucien Bouchard in place as the Canadian Ambassador to France to ensure the success of their plan to separate Quebec from Canada FAILED.

Why did these powerful people and corporations fail? Because they did not think their plan through. They were not thorough when they failed to see that, in Canada there was and still is a WILD CARD. Do not say WHAT is the wild card but rather WHO is the wild card. None other than our aboriginal population. Those who never go out and vote come election time. But when the time came to vote for the REFERENDUM the aboriginal communities came out in droves, threw their hats in the ring and VOTED.

I must also give CUDOS to thousands of Canadians who are real patriots and were so appalled at Jean Chretien's silence, transformed the planned victory for separation into a A DECISION AGAINST SEPARATION.

Both patriot Canadians and Aboriginals SAVED THE DAY.

INTEGRATION OF CANADA AND THE U.S. BY 2005

1. **The Prime Minister knows it is coming. Just look at the huge Reserve Fund in the EIC.**

2. **Disappearance of Canadian Symbols:**

   ❖ **CBC Broadcasting Corporation. (Decline of funding)**

   ❖ **Sale of the RCMP IMAGERY to Walt Disney Inc.**

   ❖ **Financial NEGLECT of our Canadian Armed Forces**

   ❖ **The DEMONIZATION of our Canadian Armed Forces**

❖ The Canadian $ (Plans to adopt US currency by Canada)

❖ Privatization & Harmonization of our MEDICARE

❖ Unnecessary savaging of our public servants (in order to dismantle our federal institutions)

❖ U.S. speakers in Ottawa. Speakers on the subject of "The Integration of Canada into the U.S." are on the scene in Ottawa to discuss the subject openly.

3. **Bother to take a closer look at the Financial Pages of the Stock market in your local daily newspaper and you will see the takeover of Canada by large U.S. corporations. Here are just a few examples: Our heritage corporation, The Hudson Bay Company sold out ZELLERS to American owned "TARGET" stores. Remember Kresge's and K-Mart all turned into American owned WAL-MART stores.**

The Separation of Quebec:

A deception of the Financiers
To take over all of Canada

It is in the best interest of the powerful corporations and in the interest of financial interests in Canada to create and foster conflicts between English and French Canadians in order to bring about the separation of Quebec. Amongst the documents that I had access to it was made very clear by the Americans that they were not interested in a merger with Canada unless Quebec separated from the rest of the country. The document went as far as stating that it had to occur in such a way that once Quebec separated from the rest of Canada, the other Canadian provinces would have no other choice but to join the United States of America and form a new alliance with the American States.

The creation of a single country in North America is a step planned by the Financiers to reach their ultimate goal of having a one world government. It involves three major economic areas in the world today: Europe, North America and the Far East (Japan, South Korea, Taiwan, Singapore, etc.) If, under the pretext of having to join forces to be able to face economic competition with the two other regions, the member countries of each of these three regions decide to merge into one single country, forming three super States. This is what is being promoted by the Trilateral Commission. The aim is to harmonize the political, economic, social and cultural relations between the three principal economic regions in the world. That is where the title of the Trilateral Commission emanated from.

Their goal has almost been achieved in Europe with the Single European Act that came into force in 1993. All members have abolished their trade barriers. In North America that has been achieved by adding to the FTA, the Free Trade Agreement between Canada and the U.S. an agreement titled NAFTA, the North American Free Trade Agreement; an agreement between the U.S., Mexico and Canada.

I am certain that most Canadians can understand that a sovereign Quebec would be no match for its humongous American neighbor. In order to survive Quebec would have to agree to merge with the U.S. This would mean the death of the French language.

It is obvious that this merger would be disastrous to all Canadians, not only Quebecers.

EVIDENCE IS EVERYWHERE

If you ignore it and you do not take action you will be personally responsible for bringing about a lifetime of misery and poverty for yourself, your family, your children and your grandchildren.

JOIN ME AND TOGETHER WE WILL MAKE A DIFFERENCE. I sincerely believe that the love most Canadians share for Canada for their community and their family creates an energy field that no one can destroy.

DO YOU REALLY WANT THE LIFE OF A SERF FOR YOURSELF AND YOUR FAMILY?

Shelley Ann Clark

Chapter 13

Meeting with the Public Service Alliance of Canada

On July 22, 1988, I believed that the only safe place that I could report the clandestine activities that had taken place at the Free Trade Negotiations Office (TNO) was to my union, the Public Service Alliance of Canada (PSAC). I therefore proceeded to file a complaint in the form of a detailed report covering the entire period of time that I had witnessed the covert activities implemented by Germain Denis since the fall of 1986.

PSAC scheduled a meeting for July 28, 1988 for 8:00 a.m. EST. I had requested to meet with my union representative, Ms. Mary Ramsay, but I was told that because my complaint was against someone who was senior management and high profile, I would be meeting a Mr. Lloyd Fucile, 2nd in command to the President, Darryl Bean.

Feeling totally secure, because I believed that PSAC would take appropriate action and report the matter to the RCMP, I entered Mr. Fucile's office without apprehension. To my astonishment there were three people sitting in with Mr. Fucile, Dennis McCarthy, representing the Staff Relations Board, Mary Ramsay as my union representative and a third person, whose name I do not recall.

I was told to proceed with what I had to report. I then handed over my typewritten report that provided the details of my disclosure. I began with my explosive information of what I had been ordered to do by Germain Denis and all the corruption that had taken place at the Trade Negotiations Office and how my life and career had been threatened if I ever told anyone.

For about 5 minutes, there was complete chaos as all three people went into a babble mode. All I kept hearing throughout this babble was "what are we going to do with this information; this is too explosive for us to handle. We had better take this matter to the President."

Finally, Mr. Fucile took charge and said "Shelley Ann, there is no point in going on with this meeting. We will take this matter to the President and let him decide what to do with it. You go home and wait for us to contact you."

I felt very frustrated with their response and insisted that they let me explain why I had come to my union. I gave them the following reasons: a) that I believed PSAC to be a safe haven for me to expose what I had witnessed and that I believed they could protect me from harm and b) that I expected them to ask the RCMP to fully investigate the corruption that had taken place and the threats to my life. After my diatribe, I then agreed to go home and wait for their call.

You can imagine my shock when by noon the next day, my doorbell rang and it was a courier service handing me an envelope with the return address indicating that it was from my union.

I had a further shock when I opened up the envelope and found my report inside with a covering letter from my union representative, Mary Ramsay.

In her letter she states ". . . . and I suggest that it should be destroyed."

On the following page is an image of the afore-mentioned covering letter dated July 29, 1988. I scanned this letter in order for you to see with your own eyes, how PSAC handled my case.

ÉLÉMENT
NATIONAL
COMPONENT

233 rue Gilmour Street,
Suite 301,
Ottawa, Ont.
K2P 0P2

(613) 560-4364

File:
Dossier: 70125/GR

HAND DELIVERED   July 29, 1988
CONFIDENTIAL

Ms. Shelley Ann Clark
505 St. Laurent Blvd. Stc.2202
OTTAWA, Ontario
K1K 3X4

Dear Sister Clark:

RE: RETURN OF DOCUMENT

        This will confirm my stated intention, during our phone
conversation of July 28, 1988 to return the above noted document.
Accordingly, it is attached to this letter and I suggest that it
should be destroyed.

        As also stated: no copies have been made. Information
necessary for the presentation of your grievance has been
extracted, in note form.

        May I again advise caution with the subject document.
It could be extremely damaging to both parties were it to fall
into the wrong hands.

                              Fraternally,

                              Mary W. Ramsay
                              Service Officer

MWR/sr

PSAC LETTER DATED JULY 29, 1988

RE: RETURN OF DOCUMENT

Chapter 14

March 28, 1989 Hearing

Prior to this March 1989 Labour Relations Board Hearing, Germain Denis retained a lawyer from the Ottawa law firm of Nelligan-Power. Mr. Denis was asked to provide his lawyer, the Department of Foreign Affairs and International Trade, my union, PSAC and the Labour Relations Board with a report providing an account of the events from his perspective.

In his report, Denis admits to his sexual advances and actually states: "It was a pressure cooker environment" giving this as a reason to excuse his behavior. Denis also said that I had also used my sexual tools to entice him. Everyone who read this report totally cracked up and could not stop laughing? They all asked the same question, what tools? Certainly not the way I dressed. Every witness could testify to the fact that I always dressed with a skirt down to my ankles with a blouse closed at the neck area as the blouses I wore had high collars with a broach.

On the day of the Labour Relations Board meeting I arrived at the appointed hearing room early and therefore was not surprised when I did not see Denis there. At the appointed hour, a well-dressed gentleman entered the room who was obviously a lawyer. It became clear to me that Denis was not going to show up.

Once the panel settled in, the first item on the agenda was where is Mr. Germain Denis? The lawyer stood up and said, Mr. Denis has asked me to represent him here today. Since Mr. Denis believes that he is only a witness and not the subject of this grievance he has made the decision to proceed to travel to Geneva, Switzerland to attend meetings. After providing everyone with the above-noted report how could the lawyer state, on behalf of Denis that Denis did not believe he was the subject of this grievance. Many were upset at this outrageous statement.

The Labour Relations Board made the immediate decision to reschedule the hearing for the month of June 1989. When I stepped outside, to my surprise there were several reporters waiting for me.

On Wednesday, March 29, 1989, the very next day, after the very brief hearing, in the morning edition of the Ottawa Citizen appeared an article by staff writer, Bert Hill. This article was strategically located in their Editorial Section immediately under Brian Mulroney's picture with the headline **"PM to meet Bush".**

The article focused on the following points:

A complaint of sexual harassment filed against one of Canada's top trade negotiators by his former secretary will be heard by the Public Service Staff Relations Board in June.

In her complaint, Shelley Ann Clark alleges she was the target of sexual harassment and discrimination over the 27 months she worked for Germain Denis, Assistant Deputy Minister for multi-lateral trade, as his Executive Assistant.

She was transferred to another job in External Affairs after lodging a complaint in July 88. Proceedings in the complaints were adjourned Tuesday.

Denis, who was involved in negotiating Canada's free-trade pact with the United States, was not present for Tuesday's proceedings.

His lawyer, John Nelligan, said Denis was heading to Geneva to participate in international trade talks.

"It will be our position that this was a high pressure operation." Nelligan said. "There was nothing personal intended".

No details of the complaint have been released. Documents filed with the staff relations board state the grievances involve both general and sexual harassment of Clark by Denis.

Nelligan said he asked for an adjournment because Denis believed he would only be a witness and not the subject of the grievance. Denis believed the complaint had been cleared up in an internal investigation, a year earlier.

But, Young said the staff relations board had clearly indicated Denis was the subject of the grievance when it notified the department of the hearing.

Dennis McCarthy, representing the Public Service Alliance of Canada, said the case should proceed because the assistant deputy minister had clearly made his decision to go to Geneva rather than attend the hearing.

Board member Roger Young agreed to give both sides the five days they need to present their arguments in June.

Clark was the subject of controversy in 1981 when then Liberal cabinet minister Lloyd Axworthy was accused of pressuring the advisory council on the status of women to drop a conference on the constitution. Clark's minutes of the council meeting showed Axworthy appeared to interfere in the council's decision. She, and then council president, Doris Anderson, quit in protest.

The staff relations board is a quasi-judicial body that hears grievances by public servants and can impose penalties.

You will note that the focus of the article was not on the wrong doings and the corruption that took place at the Trade Negotiations Office. The focus was totally on the part of my report that mentioned that throughout the negotiations Germain Denis had made sexual advances.

———

Why did the Ottawa Citizen strictly focus on the sexual harassment portion of my lengthy report? If we had an "independent press", the Ottawa Citizen would have reported the most significant sections of my report; the sections that Canadians, as citizens of Canada, had the right to know.

Chapter 23 that deals with my meeting with the RCMP in the office of Jack Ramsay, Reform MP from Alberta you will begin to understand the "control" everyone was under. No more "Freedom of Speech" as guaranteed in our Constitution and no more "independent press" and certainly NO PROTECTION for anyone reporting that our country had been sold.

Chapter 15

Meeting between the Prime Minister of Canada And the Public Service Alliance of Canada

Following the March 29, 1989 Ottawa Citizen article published in their Editorial Page under the headline "Sexual harassment complaint against trade negotiator to be heard in June" it was reported to me by Mr. Lloyd Fucile, 2nd in command of the Public Service Alliance of Canada that he had been contacted by one of Mulroney's aides and was ordered to meet with Prime Minister Brian Mulroney in his office in the Centre Block of Parliament Hill. According to Mr. Fucile, the Prime Minister had seen the Ottawa Citizen's article and wanted to have all the details surrounding the case.

The section of my report that the Ottawa Citizen focused on was the sexual harassment. What the Citizen did not report was the fact that during the two years of negotiations, in addition to Denis' sexual harassment, there had been clandestine meetings and detrimental corrupt activities that sold Canada to the Americans.

According to Mr. Fucile, when the Prime Minister heard the details of my complaint, he could not believe that Germain Denis and the Department of Foreign Affairs had jeopardized the Free Trade Agreement and the Canadian economy.

Mr. Fucile also reported that when he advised the Prime Minister that Germain Denis had also annulled my promotion, Mulroney proceeded to contact the Department of Foreign Affairs and ordered them to proceed with the promotion immediately. The Department of Foreign Affairs, in their infinite wisdom, believed that they were more powerful than the P.M. and did not comply with his order. The consequences were extremely severe as 7 heads rolled onto the proverbial carpet that day at Foreign Affairs.

Brian Mulroney ran this country like a business. He did not govern Canada as others had. Former Prime Ministers had run Canada with a humanitarian emphasis in their style like one would run a Human Rights or Charitable Organization. No. Brian Mulroney was a highly intelligent and highly successful business man and he ran this country as he would any business venture. All for maximized profit.

Therefore, can you imagine how the Prime Minister felt when he found out that one of his top negotiators had jeopardized the success of his most profitable business venture of his career, a "FREE" Trade Agreement with one of the world's most powerful country, the United States of America.

In the fall of 1999 I, for one, was certainly not surprised when I came across Germain Denis' Human Resources File that indicated that his services with the Canadian Government had been terminated several years earlier. According to all the officials I spoke to at Foreign Affairs, Mr. Denis was unable to find any work in Canada nor was he able to find work in non-governmental organizations located in French countries in Western Europe.

Finding employment in a francophone country was important to him and his family as his wife and children were unilingual at that time. Reportedly, he eventually landed a job with a small non-governmental organization in London, England.

Can you blame Brian Mulroney? I certainly don't. He used his intelligence to run this country, not his hormones. He kept "tricky dicky" under control.

Chapter 16

A Third World Country?
"The Meeting that Never Took Place"

After my union, the Public Service Alliance of Canada, met with the Prime Minister, it was reported to me that Mulroney would be demanding two things from the Department of Foreign Affairs and International Trade.

One, that they immediately give me the promotion that Germain Denis had denied me for refusing sexual favors and two, that I be assigned outside of Canada for at least 8 years.

Foreign Affairs, in its infinite wisdom, believing that they were more powerful than the Prime Minister, contravened his orders.

First, they categorically refused to give me the promotion that I had been promised and earned.

Their next step was to get the Director of Human Resources to contact me and arrange for a "special" meeting in one of their boardrooms. I was then advised not to tell anyone that this meeting was taking place.

I agreed to the meeting. When I arrived in the boardroom, there was only one person in the room; it was the Director of Human Resources, and he had set up a large screen to show me some slides.

Once I sat down, the Director informed me that he had been given the authority to offer me an ambassadorship to one of the very small third world countries. He was there to brief me on the options that I had.

I was then informed that, in that position, I would be entitled to a large home with a staff of local domestics as well as a limousine with a chauffeur and gardener. When I asked if I could bring my own staff to be chosen from Ottawa or England, I was told this was not possible because the local staff was trained in preparing the food in a certain way. When I asked why this was so essential, it was explained to me that unless all food was prepared by people who knew what concoctions to use, one could die from poisoning. According to the Director, the locals specialized in this area. One mistake in the preparation of your food and you were a goner.

The next horrifying fact was that diplomats going on assignment in those countries had official bribery money. The Treasury Board Secretariat in Ottawa saw to it because all of our food came from Canada and was brought to us once a month on a Canadian airplane. The tricky part came when he told me that the minute the airplane would land, it would be taken over by that country's military. We had to use our official bribe money to pay these soldiers to get our food off our Canadian aircraft.

If you ran out of food before the aircraft was due again, you either did without or tried to barter with a fellow Canadian. For example, if I had too many eggs left over and my colleague was out of eggs but had lots of butter left over, we could make a trade.

Therefore, you see how far FREE trade goes! The Director kept showing me slides of the various ambassadorial homes and informing me of all the fringe benefits that would be in place for me.

After approximately two hours of looking at slides and listening to the high powered marketing strategies used by the Director for me to accept one of these postings, I was more determined than ever not to accept.

I realized how easy it would be to make my death look accidental. What made me so suspicious was the fact that if our food came from Canada and was brought to us by a Canadian airplane, why was it so essential to have a local do all the preparatory work to make it safe?

As we walked back towards our respective offices, the Director kept applying pressure for me to accept an assignment to one of these third world countries. When I stood firm on my decision, I was then told "not to bother telling anyone about our meeting in the boardroom because **"IT NEVER TOOK PLACE"**.

When I realized how serious the situation was for me, I contacted my union and asked for their help to get Foreign Affairs to send me to a western world country where I believed I would be safe. It took my union one year to reach an agreement with Foreign Affairs and the involvement of a lawyer from the Treasury Board Secretariat of Canada to finally arrive at an agreement that was acceptable. I did not know at the time how wrong I was and what dangers lay ahead.

After one year of deliberations, it was agreed that I would go on assignment to Vienna, Austria for one year and then on to the Permanent Mission of Canada to the United Nations in Geneva, Switzerland for possibly another five to eight years.

The harassment that began in 1986 by Free Trade Negotiator, Germain Denis, continued throughout my assignments in Vienna, Austria and Geneva Switzerland. Eventually, the harassment became so nasty that I felt I had no choice but to return to Ottawa where I believed that I would be safe in my hometown. I was wrong. Foreign Affairs did not care that they had contravened Mulroney's orders to keep me out of the country for at lease 5 to 8 years. Foreign Affairs continued their harassment by withholding my pay checks and then declaring me a surplus employee. This last action drove me to accept a job at the Public Service Commission of Canada that led to a forced early retirement.

Believing that there was still a justice system in place and because I believed that the Canadian Human Rights Commission was an "independent body", I filed a complaint with them. I was wrong once again.

The Canadian Human Rights Commission (CHRC) and the Canadian Human Rights Tribunal (CHRT) that claim to be "independent bodies", are actually accountable to, and report to the Federal Cabinet Minister of the Federal Department of Justice. When both the CHRC and the CHRT failed to bring me justice, I appealed their decision at the JUST-US system of the Federal Court.

The complete details surrounding the harassment by Foreign Affairs, and the Public Service Commission of Canada; the injustices committed by the Chairman of the CHRT during the hearing and the unjust decision rendered and finally, the unfair decision rendered by the Judge at the Federal Court will be exposed in my next book "FIGHTING SHADOWS"—Volume II.

Chapter 17

BILL S-6: Public Service Whistleblowing Act Died In 2001

Because Bill S-6 died in 2001 I was never protected and had to suffer the repercussions for having blown the whistle. At the time, I did not even think of the consequences. All I cared about was to warn Canadians that we had been sold down the proverbial tube and sent out to sea in a canoe without the paddles.

The following has been taken from a parliamentary website: www.parl.gc.ca/common bills.

In light of the current very limited protection for whistleblowers at common law, it is arguable that there is a strong need for legislative protection at both the federal and provincial levels. At the federal level, Bill S-6, as drafted, would apply to Public Service employees but would not cover parliamentary employees, since they are not part of the federal Public Service.

If Bill S-6 were enacted into law, Canada would be following the lead of a number of other jurisdictions that already have legislation to protect public sector whistleblowers. The United States was one of the first jurisdictions to enact such legislation. At the federal level, Congress enacted the *Civil Service Reform Act* of 1978, which was subsequently amended by the *Whistleblower Protection Act of 1989*. Many U.S. States have also enacted specific whistleblower protection statutes, primarily for public sector employees, but in some cases for private sector employees also.

A very recent example of whistleblower protection legislation in a Commonwealth jurisdiction came into force in Britain on 2 July 1999 in the form of the *Public Interest Disclosure Act*. The Act generally protects both public and private sector workers who "blow the whistle" against being dismissed or penalized by their employers as a result.

Australia is another example of a Commonwealth jurisdiction that has legislation on the subject. At the federal level, through provisions of the Public Service Regulations, public service employees who report breaches or alleged breaches of the Australian Public Service Code of Conduct are protected against victimization and discrimination. The regulations also set minimum requirements for the procedures that agency heads must establish for the reporting and investigation of whistleblowing disclosures. Several States in Australia have also adopted legislation on the subject; for example, South Australia has enacted the *Whistleblowers Protection Act* 1993, and New South Wales has enacted the *Protected Disclosures Act* 1994.

According to a newspaper report, a number of Senators and MPs were supportive of Bill S-6.

Bill S-6 is introduced as a Private Senator's Public bill on January 31, 2001 in the Senate by the Hon. Noel Kinsella in the 2nd Session of the 36th Parliament, but died on the Order Paper with the dissolution of Parliament.

If the United States, the U.K. and Australia have protection for whistleblowers why does Canada not follow suit?

We should be asking the Prime Minister of Canada why we are still living in the dark ages when it comes to this issue, and why is the importance of this issue being ignored?

LS-384E

BILL S-6: PUBLIC SERVICE WHISTLEBLOWING ACT

Prepared by:
David Johansen
Law and Government Division
5 February 2001

LEGISLATIVE HISTORY OF BILL S-6

HOUSE OF COMMONS		SENATE	
Bill Stage	**Date**	**Bill Stage**	**Date**
First Reading:		First Reading:	31 January 2001
Second Reading:		Second Reading:	31 January 2001
Committee Report:		Committee Report:	28 March 2001
Report Stage:		Report Stage:	29 March 2001
Third Reading:		Third Reading:	

<table>
<tr><td colspan="3">Royal Assent:
Statutes of Canada</td></tr>
<tr><td colspan="3">N.B. Any substantive changes in this Legislative Summary which have been made since the preceding issue are indicated in bold print.</td></tr>
<tr><td></td><td></td><td></td></tr>
</table>

TABLE OF CONTENTS

BILL S-6: PUBLIC SERVICE
WHISTLEBLOWING ACT

BACKGROUND

A. Introduction

On 31 January 2001, a Private Senator's Public bill, Bill S-6, the Public Service Whistleblowing Act, was introduced in the Senate by the Hon. Noel Kinsella. (1) The bill received second reading on the same date and was referred to the Standing Senate Committee on National Finance. The bill would establish a mechanism for dealing with the reporting of wrongdoing in the federal Public Service. Although federally to date there have been no government bills on the subject, a number of Private Members' bills have been introduced in the House of Commons. For example, Bill C-293, an Act to amend the Canadian Human Rights Act, the Canada Labour Code and the Public Service Employment Act (whistleblowing) (3rd Session, 34th Parliament) was introduced in the House of Commons by Ms. Joy Langan on 24 September 1991. It was later debated at second reading and dropped from the *Order Paper*. A virtually identical Private Member's bill, Bill C-248, was introduced in the House by Mr. Pierre de Savoye on 11 May 1994 (1st Session, 35th Parliament). This bill also was subsequently debated at second reading and dropped from the *Order Paper*. A later and different Private Member's bill on the subject was introduced in the House by Mr. de Savoye on 19 June 1996; this bill, Bill C-318, Whistle Blowers Protection Act (2nd Session, 35th Parliament) died with the dissolution of Parliament, having received only first reading. Bill C-499, a similar Private Member's bill with some additional provisions, was introduced in the House by Mr. Pat Martin on 23 April 1999 (1st Session, 36th Parliament) but did not go beyond first reading. It was subsequently re-introduced as Bill C-239 in the House by Mr. Martin on 18 October 1999 (2nd Session, 36th Parliament) but died on the *Order Paper* with the dissolution of Parliament. It was later re-introduced as Bill C-206 in the House by Mr. Martin on 2 February 2001 (1st Session, 37th Parliament). Another Private Member's bill, Bill C-508, Whistle Blower Human Rights Act, was introduced in the House by Mr. Gurmant Grewal on 17 October 2000 (2nd Session, 36th Parliament). It died on the *Order Paper* with the dissolution of Parliament. It was subsequently re-introduced as Bill C-201 in the House by Mr. Grewal on 1 February 2001 (1st Session, 37th Parliament).

As a background to discussion of Bill S-6, the following section of the paper describes the current law on whistleblowing in Canada.

B. Current Law on Whistleblowing in Canada

In Canada, as in certain other jurisdictions, most notably the United States, a number of statutes, particularly those covering environmental or occupational health and safety matters, protect employees within their jurisdiction against retaliation for having exercised certain rights conferred by the statutes. One such provision at the federal level in Canada is section 16 of the new *Canadian Environmental Protection Act, 1999*, which provides for protection against employment reprisals for employees who, in good faith, give designated officials information relating to offences under the Act.

Governments in Canada, however, at both the federal and provincial levels, have thus far generally declined to enact broader whistleblower protection legislation such as exists in certain other countries. In the United States, for example, legislation at the federal level covers federal public sector employees, while legislation in some States protects public sector workers and in some other States protects both public and private sector workers. It would appear that the only such general legislation in force in Canada is section 28 of New Brunswick's *Employment Standards Act*, which applies to employers in both the private and public sectors, and which in general provides protection against employment reprisals for employees who make complaints against their employers with respect to the alleged violation of any provincial or federal legislation.

In Ontario, section 58(6) of the *Public Service and Labour Relations Statute Law Amendment Act, 1993*, which received Royal Assent on 14 December 1993, added a new Part IV (sections 28.11 –28.43), entitled "Whistleblowers' Protection," to the *Public Service Act*, to give broad protection for public sector whistleblowers in that province. According to section 28.43 of the *Public Service Act* , however, Part IV is to come into force on a day to be named by proclamation of the Lieutenant Governor. After the legislation was enacted, however, the New Democratic Party government was replaced by a Progressive Conservative government, now in its second mandate, whose agenda does not include proclamation into force of Part IV.

In Canada, therefore, whistleblowers in both the public and private sectors are forced to rely chiefly on the protection offered by the common law. As noted in the Ontario Law Reform Commission's *Report on Political Activity, Public Comment and Disclosure by Crown Employees* (1986), under the common law an employee owes his or her employer the general duties of loyalty, good faith and, in appropriate circumstances, confidentiality. "Loyalty" embraces the obligation to perform assigned work diligently and skillfully, to refrain from any sort of deception related to the employment contract, to avoid any relationships, remunerative or otherwise, that might give rise to an interest inconsistent with that of the employer, and to conduct oneself at all times so as not to be a discredit to one's employer. "Good faith" requires an employee to perform assigned tasks according to the best interests of his or her employer. Finally, "confidentiality" may give an employee a duty to keep certain information confidential until released from that duty by the employer. This duty may arise by contract, or it may be imposed by equity whenever the employer entrusts an employee with "confidential" information on the understanding that it is not to be disclosed without authorization. A general duty of confidentiality may arise by virtue of a particular relationship between the employer and the employee.

When an employee breaches these duties and reveals a confidence or some information, believing that to do so is in the public interest, the employer routinely takes disciplinary action, which may include dismissal. In the face of such punishment, some employees have sought protection from the courts or, if they are governed by a collective agreement, through a grievance procedure.

When the wrongdoing has been serious and the public's interest in disclosure is clear, the courts have permitted a very limited "public interest" defence in these cases. They have emphasized the need for the employee to use internal remedies first, to be sure of the facts and to exercise good judgment in his or her actions. Arbitrators have applied similar criteria. In general, it may be said that employees have at present only a narrow range of protection and may seriously jeopardize their careers by breaching their duties to their employers.

The Professional Institute of the Public Service of Canada (PIPSC), a national union representing some 36,000 professional and scientific employees, has for some years been calling upon the federal government to enact legislation to protect federal public sector employees from potential reprisals for "blowing the whistle." The Public Service Alliance of Canada (PSAC), representing over 150,000 federal public servants and employees of agencies,

Crown corporations and the territories, has also recommended enactment of such legislation.

DESCRIPTION AND ANALYSIS

A. Purpose of the Bill

Bill S-6 would be entitled the Public Service Whistleblowing Act (clause 1). Its purpose, set out in clause 2, would be:

- to educate Public Service employees on ethical practices in the workplace and to promote the observance of those practices;

- to provide a means for Public Service employees to make allegations of wrongful acts or omissions in the workplace, in confidence, to an independent Commissioner who would investigate them and seek to have the situation dealt with and who would report to Parliament in respect of confirmed problems that had not been dealt with; and

- to protect Public Service employees from retaliation for having made or for proposing to make, in good faith and on the basis of reasonable belief, allegations of wrongdoing in the workplace.

B. Interpretation

Clause 3 would define a number of terms for purposes of the bill. The "Commissioner" would mean a commissioner of the Public Service Commission designated as the Public Interest Commissioner under clause 4, while an "employee" would mean a person who was an employee within the meaning of the *Public Service Employment Act;* i.e., a person appointed to the Public Service under the authority of the Public Service Commission where "Public Service" refers to the positions in or under any department or other portion of the Public Service of Canada specified in Schedule 1 to the *Public Service Staff Relations Act.* Similarly, under the bill, the "Public Service" would mean the parts of the Public Service covered by the *Public Service Staff Relations Act.* A "law in force in Canada" would mean either a federal or provincial statute or an instrument issued under the authority of such a statute. "Minister" would mean a federal Cabinet Minister. A "wrongful act or omission" would mean an act or omission that was: a) an offence under any law in force in Canada; b) likely to cause a significant waste of public money; c) likely to endanger public health or safety or the environment; d) a significant breach of an established public policy or directive in the written record of the Public Service; or e) one of gross mismanagement or abuse of authority.

C. Public Interest Commissioner

The federal Cabinet would designate one of the commissioners of the Public Service Commission to serve as Public Interest Commissioner for purposes of the bill (clause 4(1)). The Public Interest Commissioner's functions would be deemed to be within the work of the Public Service Commission for the purposes of the *Public Service Employment Act* (clause 4(2)), and the powers granted to the Commissioner by the *Public Service Employment Act* for the purposes of that Act could be exercised for purposes of the bill (clause 4(3)).

Subject to clause 10, referred to below, the Commissioner, if he or she believed it was in the public interest to do so, could make public any information that came to his or her attention as a result of performing the Commissioner's duties or powers under the bill (clause 5(1)). The Commissioner, or a person acting on the Commissioner's behalf, could disclose information that, in the Commissioner's opinion, was necessary to conduct an investigation under the bill or to establish grounds for the findings or recommendations of any report made under the bill (clause 5(2)). As well, the Commissioner, or a person acting on the Commissioner's behalf, could disclose information in the course of a prosecution for an offence under clause 21 of the bill or section 132 of the *Criminal Code* (perjury) in respect of a statement made under the bill (clause 5(3)). The Commissioner would also be empowered to disclose to the Attorney General of Canada, or of any province, information relating to the commission of an offence against any law in force in Canada of which the Commissioner had uncovered evidence during the exercise of his or her duties or powers under the bill (clause 5(4)).

The Commissioner, or a person acting on the Commissioner's behalf, would not be regarded as a competent witness in respect of any matter that came to his or her knowledge in the performance of the Commissioner's duties or powers under the bill other than in a prosecution for an offence under clause 21 of the bill or section 132 of the *Criminal Code* (perjury) in respect of a statement made under the bill (clause 6).

No criminal or civil proceedings would be taken against the Commissioner, or a person acting on the Commissioner's behalf, for anything done, reported or said in good faith in performing the Commissioner's duties or powers under the bill (clause 7(1)). For the purposes of any libel or slander law, anything said, any information supplied, or any record or thing produced in good faith and on the basis of reasonable belief in the course of an investigation carried out by or on behalf of the Commissioner under the bill would be privileged, as would be any report made in good faith by the Commissioner under the bill and any fair and accurate account of the report made in good faith for purposes of news reporting (clause 7(2)).

The Commissioner would be required to promote ethical practices in the Public Service and to foster a positive environment for giving notice of wrongdoing by disseminating information about the bill and by such other means as he or she found fit (clause 8).

D. Notice of Wrongful Act or Dismissal

A Public Service employee who believed that another Public Service employee had committed or intended to commit a wrongful act or omission could file a written notice of the allegation with the Commissioner and could request that his or her own identity be kept confidential (clause 9(1)). The notice would have to identify the employee making the allegation, the person against whom the allegation was being made, and the grounds for the allegation (clause 9(2)). Such notice given in good faith and on the basis of reasonable belief would not be deemed to constitute a breach of any oath of office or loyalty or secrecy taken by the employee and, subject to clause 9(4), not to be a breach of duty (clause 9(3)). In giving notice under clause 9(1), no employee, unless prompted by reasonable concerns for public health or safety, would be permitted to violate any law in force in Canada or any rule of law protecting privileged communications between solicitor and client (clause 9(4)).

Subject to any requirement imposed on the Commissioner under the bill or any law in force in Canada, the Commissioner would be required to keep confidential the identity of the employee who had filed the notice of allegation and who had been given the Commissioner's assurance of such confidentiality (clause 10).

Pursuant to clause 9, the Commissioner would have to review a notice of allegation and could ask the employee for further information and make such further inquiries as were considered necessary (clause 11).

The Commissioner would reject, and take no further action on, a notice of allegation where he or she had made a preliminary determination that the notice was trivial, frivolous or vexatious; failed to allege or give adequate particulars of a wrongful act or omission; breached clause 9(4); or had not been given in good faith or on the basis of reasonable belief (clause 12(1)). The Commissioner could determine that a notice of allegation had not been given in good faith if it contained a statement that the employee, at the time of making it, had known to be false or misleading (clause 12(2)). However, the Commissioner would not have to make such determination solely because the allegation contained mistaken facts (clause 12(3)). The Commissioner would be required to communicate his or her determination under clause 12(1) in writing, and on a timely basis, to the employee who had given the notice (clause 12(4)). As well, where the Commissioner determined under clause 12(1) that a notice had been given in breach of clause 9(4) or without good faith and on the basis of reasonable belief, he or she could so advise the person against whom the allegation was made and the Minister responsible for the employee who had given the notice (clause 12(5)).

The Commissioner would be required to accept a notice of allegation that he or she determined was not trivial, frivolous or vexatious; did allege and give adequate particulars of a wrongful act or omission; did not breach clause 9(4); and had been made in good faith and on the basis of reasonable belief (clause 13(1)). In such a case, the Commissioner would also be required, in writing and on a timely basis, so to advise the employee who had filed the notice (clause 13(2)).

E. Investigation and Report

The Commissioner would investigate a notice of allegation accepted under clause 13(1) and would have to prepare a written report of findings and recommendations (clause 14(1)) except if satisfied that: the employee ought to first exhaust other review procedures; the matter could more appropriately be dealt with, initially or completely, through a procedure provided for under another statute; or the length of time between the wrongful act or omission and the date the notice had been filed was such that a report would not serve a useful purpose (clause 14(2)). Where no written report was required, the Commissioner, in writing and on a timely basis, would have to so advise the employee who had filed the notice of allegation (clause 14(3)). Where the Commissioner produced a written report, however, he or she would be required to provide, on a timely basis, a copy of this to the Minister responsible for the employee against whom the allegation was made (clause 14(4)).

After considering such a report, a Minister would have to notify the Commissioner of what action had or would be taken (clause 15(2)). In the case of proposed action, the Minister would be required to give such further responses "as seem[ed] appropriate to the Commissioner" until such time as the Minister advised that the matter had been dealt with (clause 15(3)).

If, in the Commissioner's opinion, it was in the public interest, he or she could prepare an emergency report and require the President of the Treasury Board to have this submitted to Parliament on the next day that either House sat (clause 16(1)). The emergency report would have to describe the substance of a report made to a Minister under clause 14(4) and the Minister's response or lack of response under clause 15 (clause 16(2)).

The Public Service Commission would be required to include in its annual report to Parliament (made pursuant to section 47 of the *Public Service Employment Act*) a statement of activity under this bill, prepared by the Public Interest Commissioner and including the information spelled out in clause 17(1) of the bill. The report could also include an analysis of the administration and operation of the bill and any further recommendations of the Commission (clause 17(2)).

F. Prohibitions

No person could take any disciplinary action against a Public Service employee who, acting in good faith and on the basis of reasonable belief: a) had disclosed or stated an intention to disclose to the Public Interest Commissioner that another Public Service employee had committed a wrongful act or omission; b) had refused or stated an intention to refuse to commit an act or omission that would contravene the bill; or c) had done or stated an intention to do something required in order to comply with the bill (clause 19(1)). Neither would a person be permitted to take any disciplinary action against an employee who he or she believed would do any of the above (clause 19(1)). "Disciplinary action" would mean any action that might adversely affect the employee or any term or condition of the employee's employment; it would include harassment, financial penalty, any action affecting seniority, suspension or dismissal, denial of meaningful work, demotion, denial of a benefit of employment, or an action that was otherwise disadvantageous to the employee (clause 19(2)). A person who took disciplinary action contrary to clause 19 within two years after an employee had given a notice of allegation to the Commissioner under clause 9(1) would be presumed, in the absence of a preponderance of evidence to the contrary, to have done so because the employee had given the notice (clause 19(3)).

Except as authorized by the bill or any other law in force in Canada, clause 20(1) would prohibit disclosure of the existence or nature of a notice of allegation given by a Public Service employee to the Commissioner under clause 9(1) in such a way as to identify the employee who had made it. There would be an exception where a notice had been given in breach of clause 9(4) or not in good faith and on the basis of reasonable belief (clause 20(2)).

G. Enforcement

A person who contravened clause 9(4), 18, 19(1), or 20(1) of the bill would be guilty of an offence and liable on summary conviction to a fine not exceeding $10,000 (clause 21).

H. Employee Recourse

An employee against whom disciplinary action was taken contrary to clause 19 would be entitled to use every legal recourse available, including grievance proceedings provided for under a federal statute or otherwise (clause 22(1)). An employee could seek such recourse regardless of whether criminal proceedings based upon the same facts were or might be brought under clause 21 (clause 22(2)). In all recourse proceedings referred to in clause 22(1), an employee would be entitled to the benefit of the presumption in clause 19(3) (clause 22(3)). Grievance proceedings pending on the coming into force of the bill would be dealt with and disposed of as if the bill had not been enacted (clause 22(4)).

COMMENTARY

According to a newspaper report,(2) a number of Senators and M.P.s are supportive of Bill S-6.

In light of the current very limited protection for whistleblowers at common law, it is arguable that there is a strong need for legislative protection at both the federal and provincial levels. At the federal level, Bill S-6, as drafted, would apply to Public Service employees but would not cover parliamentary employees, since these are not part of the federal Public Service.

If Bill S-6 were enacted into law, Canada would be following the lead of a number of other jurisdictions that already have legislation to protect public sector whistleblowers. The United States was one of the first jurisdictions to enact such legislation. At the federal level, Congress enacted the *Civil Service Reform Act of 1978*, which was subsequently amended by the *Whistleblower Protection Act of 1989*. Many U.S. States have also enacted specific whistleblower protection statutes, primarily for public sector employees, but in some cases for private sector employees also.

A very recent example of whistleblower protection legislation in a Commonwealth jurisdiction came into force in Britain on 2 July 1999 in the form of the *Public Interest Disclosure Act*. The Act generally protects both public and private sector workers who "blow the whistle" against being dismissed or penalized by their employers as a result.

Australia is another example of a Commonwealth jurisdiction that has legislation on the subject. At the federal level, through provisions of the *Public Service Regulations*, public service employees who report breaches or alleged breaches of the Australian Public Service Code of Conduct are protected against victimization and discrimination. The regulations also set minimum requirements for the procedures that agency heads must establish for the reporting and investigation of whistleblowing disclosures. Several States in Australia have also adopted legislation on the subject; for example, South Australia has enacted the *Whistleblowers Protection Act 1993*, and New South Wales has enacted the *Protected Disclosures Act 1994*.

---

(1) The bill is virtually identical to Bill S-13 which was introduced in the Senate by the Hon. Noel Kinsella in the 2nd Session of the 36th Parliament but died on the *Order Paper* with the dissolution of Parliament.

(2) "MPs like Senators' Whistle-blowing bill," *Ottawa Citizen*, 3 February 2001.

Chapter 18

The Manipulation of Canadian History

This photograph is attributed to
Padraic Ryan

The views and opinions expressed in this book in no way reflect the views and opinions of Mr. Ryan.

LIBRARY & ARCHIVES CANADA BUILDING

As most of you know, with today's technology, the hard copy of news papers are not kept in a warehouse like in the old days.

Today, they are put onto microfiche which anyone can view in the Library of Archives Canada.

In this case, it involved an article that appeared in the Ottawa Citizen on March 29, 1989 titled "Sexual harassment case against top trade negotiator to be heard in June". This article, written by Citizen Staff Writer, Bert Hill appeared on the Citizen's Editorial page right underneath the picture of Prime Minister, Brian Mulroney. When I went to Archives Canada to retrieve a copy of this article from the microfiche imagine my surprise when it had completely vanished. Someone had replaced it with an ad for men's clothing.

When I, and my witness, John Richard Bowlby asked an employee of Archives Canada what happened to it, I was asked "Are you sure that you have the right date and the right paper?" When the employee was advised who I was and was shown my diplomatic passport and special research ID, as well as being the subject of the article, she believed there was no mistake on my part. She told me that they were keeping all hard copies of the Ottawa Citizen in their warehouse and that she could order it to be delivered to her by the next morning. That is how I managed to obtain the correct original version. You wanted evidence of tampering. There it is.

By approximately 10:00 a.m. the next morning, when my Campaign Manager, John Bowlby and I arrived at Archives Canada we quickly took the newspaper and opened it to the editorial section. John and I were absolutely shocked when he made the comparison between the microfiche version and the hard copy version.

We were both devastated to realize that Canadians could not even trust their own Archives Library. It was a chilling thought, that generations in the future, doing research on their country, could not rely on any information that they would find in their own archives. Had the Prime Minister achieved the manipulation of historical events of our country? As we stood there gaping at the enormity of our discovery, we suddenly realized and understood what the Prime Minister meant when he gave his farewell speech as he was leaving the political arena. He stated, "I know that future generations will be a better judge of me . . . ."

YES, suddenly IT all made sense. At the time, when I was listening and watching his farewell speech on TV, it had totally baffled me on how he could state that future generations would be a better judge of him. Of course, it's simple to achieve this when you have the power to control, orchestrate and manipulate the reporting of key events that affect the well being of Canadians and their country. That was the problem with the Prime Minister, he believed he owned Canada and he believed he was God.

The evidence of tampering is clear. How can we ever trust Archives Canada again after we uncovered this manipulation? How can future generations get the true history of Canada when they go to the Library & Archives Canada to do their research, especially on key issues that affect them and their country.

I was hoping to provide my readers with a photocopy of these articles, but after contacting the responsible individual by phone at the Ottawa Citizen I was told that even though the articles were published and widely distributed to the public, which should have made it OK for me to reproduce them as long as I gave the author and the Ottawa Citizen credit for it, the answer was negative. According to the Ottawa Citizen employee, every article published in their newspaper is protected under our copyright laws and unless they give their authorization to reproduce it you are breaking the law if you do so. So much for FREEDOM in this country when information provided to the public only belongs to the Ottawa Citizen and other mainstream media.

I did not give up after the initial phone call to get permission to reproduce the morning and final evening edition. I wrote to another individual who reportedly was in charge of authorizations. You guessed it, I never received a response.

Further evidence that historical records are being tampered with in this country comes from what CBC television did to the

Honorable Paul Hellyer, former Federal Cabinet Minister for the Department of National Defence.

On the day that the Honorable Paul Hellyer launched his Canadian Action Party, CBC interviewed him on air. The interview was broadcast on the early morning edition of the National News. Guess what? It never appeared again. Not on that day; not that week, nor the following week; not in the following months. It was as if it had never occurred. It had become "de novo". Hellyer was doing a good thing for his country, but those of us who did not watch the early edition of the CBC News Broadcast never found out that he was attempting to put together another party to ensure that there was a better balance of power in Parliament. I only found out by accident, through a friend that had a video copy of Paul Hellyer's speech.

— "de novo" means NEW, AFRESH, NEVER EXISTED

Chapter 19

The Controlled Mainstream Media

Despite the fact that the Ottawa Citizen's journalist had reported my 1988 case on their editorial page, no other mainstream media touched it.

Why? Was it because all mainstream media corporations were owned by Mulroney's buddies?

Five years later, when I decided to run in the Federal election, one gutsy investigative reporter, Charlie Greenwell, who had his own segment on our local CJOH television station called "INSIDER'S REPORT", made the decision to investigate my story. After a lengthy investigation process, the CJOH legal team made the decision to allow Greenwell to interview me.

I was interviewed for 30 minutes, and Yes, you guessed right, CJOH only allowed barely 2 minutes to be aired.

But this was a very valuable 2 minutes as it was reported to me that the interview would be aired across Canada. As I only saw what was broadcast in Ottawa, I can only assume that they did so. As this broadcast resulted in guest speaking engagements and interviews across Canada and on major radio talk shows in the U.S., the interview must have aired across the country as reported. Guest speaking engagements went as far as taking me to a small town called Cache Creek located in the middle of nowhere, and at the entrance to the Yukon and the North West Territories.

Following this 2 minutes of fame, I was contacted by a young journalism student from McGill University in Montreal. This young student travelled to Ottawa and interviewed me personally at my home. His name was Alex Roslyn and as a result, because of his incredible talent, his persistence, or should I say stubbornness, this journalist went right to the source by pursuing his investigation directly with Simon Reisman and Gordon Ritchie.

On the following pages, I will share the articles that appeared in the newspaper that he worked for: "The Montreal Mirror". Unfortunately, he was so good at his job, that one day he was called in to his boss's office and was told that he had become too political and could no longer work for their paper. Alex paid a heavy price for his integrity. The last I heard, he had managed to obtain employment with a small newspaper with an aboriginal group.

All articles that follow are **replicas** that were reproduced in order to allow the publisher to input the material as part of this book "THE SALE OF A COUNTRY".

REPLICA

August 26, 1993

MONTREAL MIRROR

"MEDIA IGNORES BRIANGATE"
By
Alex Roslin

FREE TRADE CHARADE

This could be Canada's Watergate…and the majors won't touch it.

A former Free Trade Official charges five years later that her boss, a top negotiator, made her alter key documents.

Shelley Ann Clark can't get anyone in the media to listen to her story of document-altering in the Canada-U.S. free trade negotiations. Clark claims her boss, top trade negotiator Germain Denis, committed fraud to conceal what Canada gave away in the talks with the Americans.

Only one media outlet, Ottawa TV station CJOH, DID A STORY AFTER Clark went public with her story on May 26, 1993. CJOH aired a three-minute interview with Clark on June 3. Ottawa Citizen columnist Greg Watson said he heard about Clark's allegations in mid-summer, but didn't have the time to look into them. "I felt it was the sort of thing that would take a month to investigate," he said. "I just couldn't take out that kind of time".

Weston passed on the file to Citizen reporter Mark Kennedy, who told the Mirror Monday, he also didn't have enough time to look into the case. "I'm not working on it currently," he said. "It's a very difficult matter to verify, I suspect." But when asked if he had at least tried, Kennedy responded "Nope".

Stevie Cameron, whose former Globe and Mail "Influence" column often probed government corruption, has known about Clark's allegations for two months but also has not written anything "I didn't have enough to go on", she told the Mirror. "I think it's really interesting but I'd like to get more documentation." Both Clark and her lawyer, Harold Funk, said this week Cameron had yet to interview them about the case or seek any documentation.

NDP trade critic Dave Barrett said Clark's story deserves public attention. "These are serious allegations," he said, adding that he had not heard about Clark's allegations before the Mirror called. Barrett said free-trade opponents have long claimed federal officials were not above-board about what was given away in the trade talks. "The whole business of the trade negotiations—who was pulling the strings in all this—all of these things are a mystery."

REPLICA

"FREE TRADE CHARADE"
BY
ALEX ROSLIN

August 19-August 26, 1993

A former Free Trade official charges five years later that her boss, a top negotiator, made her alter key documents.

The MAN WHO was Brian Mulroney's personal contact in the office that negotiated the 1988 Canada-U.S. Free Trade Agreement is about to be investigated by the RCMP for allegedly tampering with key briefing documents during the free-trade talks.

In a stunning case of intrigue and secret nighttime liaisons, the Mounties are looking into one woman's claims that Germain Denis, a top negotiator on the team that forged the deal, shredded and altered documents intended for provincial officials that outlined the concessions Canada had made during the free trade talks.

The woman who spilled the beans, Shelley Ann Clark, was Denis' executive secretary (later given the title of Executive Assistant by Gordon Ritchie) during the talks. She told the Mirror in a five-hour interview that Denis repeatedly ordered her to go to government offices after midnight to alter the documents. In order to conceal the fraud, Denis allegedly ordered his assistant to shred classified documents and secretly remove other papers from the office and put them in his car. "WE purposefully deceived the provinces," Clark said.

Denis, the number-three man in the free trade talks, behind ambassadors Simon Reisman and Gordon Ritchie, was Mulroney's little-known point man in the federal Trade Negotiations Office, according to Clark. She said Denis had frequent direct contact with the prime minister.

Denis, currently on vacation, was unavailable for comment. His present position is assistant deputy minister of multilateral commercial trade.

During the trade talks, Denis was responsible for negotiating five vital trade areas with the Americans, and briefing the provinces on those areas—the cultural sector, subsidies, tariffs, agriculture, intellectual property and government procurement.

Clark claims her boss ordered her to alter top-secret briefing books used by Denis to give the provinces detailed accounts of Ottawa's position and strategy in the free-trade talks. The briefing books revealed what federal officials had given away or won in the talks as they unfolded.

At secret night-time sessions several times a week, Clark said Denis ordered her to delete "entire paragraphs" that outlined concessions and to alter other sections to soften the perception that Ottawa was giving away the farm.

"We were telling the provinces the free-trade talks were not touching social security programs," said Clark, a 32-year veteran of the department of External Affairs and International Trade. "In fact, we were incorporating into the American system over a number of years. It's just now that we're starting to notice some changes to social security programs. They are slowly easing the country into the changes."

Clark said the real federal positions were written into the final text of the Free Trade Agreement much later by the federal legal team. "They were able to hide it in the legal language," Clark said. Federal lawyers did not have the binding legal text ready until December 1988, more than a year after Mulroney announced the FTA to the public.

If the provinces had known what was really being given away, Clark added, more premiers may have expressed public opposition to the Free Trade Agreement and the Conservatives may not have been re-elected in the 1988 federal election.

Clark maintains that during the talks her boss repeatedly took direct calls from then prime minister Mulroney - even though Denis was only the number-three man in the talks. The calls came at odd hours - often during lunch - when no one else was around.

Provincial BRIEFING sessions occurred immediately after each stage of the discussions with the Americans, usually on a monthly basis. After each session, provincial officials had to return the briefing books. Clark claims Denis would then have her shred all but one of the 10 provincial copies of the books.

At the end of the talks, Clark said Denis had her secretly remove seven boxes full of doctored briefing books from federal offices and place them in the trunk of his car. Clark said ambassadors Reisman and Ritchie had sole authority to permit document shredding, but were not consulted by Denis.

Simon Reisman headed the free-trade talks and was given the honorary title of "ambassador". Today he is chairman of Ranger Oil. He seemed speechless when told of Clark's allegations. "Oh goodness, oh goodness," he said then paused. "As the head of the delegation, I was the man responsible for dealing with the provinces and any notion that fabricated documents were given to the provinces has got to be pure fiction," he said.

Reached at his Ottawa home, Reisman described Denis as "a very high-class senior officer" and said "every document produced for the TNO {Trade Negotiations Office} is with the archives."

Ritchie, Reisman's second-in-command and now also employed in the private sector, denied that Denis had any direct contact with the Prime Minister's Office during the trade talks. But when pressed, he said, "While I was there, he {Mulroney} would never speak with Mr. Denis without me being present."

Asked whether any provincial briefing material was destroyed, Ritchie said: "They would be considered part of the official government documents of Canada and, as such, would not be destroyed." Still, he conceded he did not know for sure whether all the material was passed on to the public archives.

Paul Martin, the National Archive's keeper of government trade documents, said he has discovered that a series of free-trade documents are indeed missing. Last week, Martin went searching for papers related to the free-trade discussions and found his file system has records of papers that are not actually present in the archives.

"It appeared we didn't have all the records," Martin said. He suggested the papers may simply be misplaced, but added that there is "no way to verify" if the Trade Negotiations Office delivered all its documents to the archives. "It's hard to say we have everything."

There is no way of inspecting the trade-related documents in the archives without a lengthy access-to-information case. In the fall of 1991, the Ottawa Citizen did an Access to Information to request papers on "culture" that had been negotiated in the Free Trade Agreement. It would take two years before the Ottawa Citizen would receive a response.

RCMP INSPECTOR Pierre Droz of the Commercial Crimes Unit interviewed Clark for 90 minutes about the allegations at the end of June this year. Droz said Monday he still had not decided whether to launch an investigation and still had to consult his superiors.

The unit's spokesman, Gerry Boucher, told a different story. He said Thursday that an investigation was definitely planned, although an investigator had yet to be assigned to the case. "It will be done sometime in early September."

The Mounties got onto the case after Clark hired renowned Ottawa civil litigator Harold Funk, who sent out packages detailing her case to the premiers and media in May 1993. (See Appendix D).

Clark decided to take her case public five years after filing a formal grievance with her union against Denis alleging sexual harassment and fraud. The grievance was settled in Clark's favor, but she claims she was hounded by Denis' allies in other jobs within the government. In December 1992, she was put on paid leave after she filed a second grievance alleging harassment and sexual harassment, this time involving a new boss. The terms of both grievance settlements are confidential.

The night-time document-altering sessions ultimately cost Clark her 16-year marriage. She claimed Denis repeatedly told her if she discussed the alterations with anyone, she would be fired. So, she kept her family in the dark. "He kept telling me if I repeated anything, I would never work in the government again," said Clark, a federal employee since 1961. "I was very scared of the knowledge I had. She claimed Denis also blocked her requests for a transfer.

Clark's 20-year-old son, Stephen, remembers his mother receiving calls after midnight "two or three times a week" requesting her to return to work. Stephen thought it was odd but assumed his mother was simply involved in late-night free-trade negotiations. "I did not know at the time [about the document-tampering]," he said.

Neither did Clark's husband, Richard (who could not be reached for comment). The couple separated in April 1988. "The marriage was completely over," said Clark. "There was no more trust."

She decided to take her case public because she believes her career has now been destroyed, just like her marriage. Funk, her lawyer, said he is preparing a lawsuit against seven government officials, including Denis and Mulroney, seeking compensation. "This is not going to die," he said. "The amount of fraud being perpetrated against the Canadian people behind closed doors is phenomenal. I've heard some outrageous things in my time. But when you sell your goddam country down the tube, that takes the cake."

Trade Official plays down harassment charges
By
Alex Roslin

September 23, 1993.

The Man who helped engineer the Canada-U.S. Free Trade Agreement admits there was sexual harassment in his office, but says the problems weren't serious enough to warrant action.

"There were all kinds of romances. That's the nature of relationships between men and women," said Simon Reisman, Canada's ambassador to the trade talks, when asked to comment on complaints of sexual harassment in his office by Shelley Ann Clark. "I must say that the whole definition of sexual harassment has become so broad now."

Apart from sexual harassment, Clark has also accused her boss, top trade negotiator Germain Denis, of ordering her to alter and shred key documents to conceal what Ottawa gave away in the trade talks. Clark was Denis' executive secretary. She filed a formal grievance against Denis in July 1988. During a March 1989 hearing into the sexual harassment charge, Denis' lawyer was quoted in an Ottawa Citizen article saying: "It will be our position that this was a high pressure operation: There was nothing personal intended."

The grievance was eventually settled in Clark's favour but she claims to have been hounded in other government jobs by Denis' allies. She was put on paid leave last December when she filed another harassment grievance. Clark claims her 32-year civil service career has been derailed.

Reisman has since left the government and is chair of Calgary-based Ranger Oil. He admitted in an interview to having heard about the sexual harassment case against Denis but says he did nothing about it. Denis currently in charge of representing Canada at the GATT talks.

REISMAN'S COMMENTS WERE BLASTED BY A CIVIL-RIGHTS GROUP IN Ottawa that has supported Clark. It's the usual story when a case surfaces publicly: denials and the attitude that boys will be boys," said John Richard Bowlby, an executive member of Citizens Against Bad Law. "These sexual advances are an abuse of power."

Bowlby's group has helped dozens of female government employees facing sexual harassment. Occasionally, the group is approached for help by someone who is lying or unstable, Bowlby said, but he is convinced that Clark is credible. "We have scrutinized her case thoroughly."

SCUTTLE
BY
Alex Roslin

September 30, 1993

HURTIG SNATCHES UP CLARK. Mel Hurtig's National Party has recruited Shelley Ann Clark as its candidate in the Ottawa riding of Carleton-Gloucester. Clark is the 32-year civil servant who claims her boss, top Canada-U.S. trade negotiator Germain Denis, ordered her to shred and alter key documents to conceal what Ottawa gave away in the Free Trade talks. Clark's registration papers were signed half an hour before the Monday deadline.

I'm finally going to get the message out to Canadians about what really happened with the Free Trade Agreement," Clark said, promising to campaign for whistle-blower protection for government workers and "a free press". The mainstream media has ignored Clark's story until this week despite months of lobbying by her lawyer and free trade opponents.

In another development, Clark claimed that she and one of her supporters have received a death threat and menacing phone calls. In early September, Clark briefly left many of her personal records with Cynthia Syms, a Wakefield, Quebec lawyer, for safe-keeping. Syms said she got repeated phone calls from individuals claiming to have Clark's authorization to pick up the documents. One identified as an RCMP inspector, another as Clark's housekeeper. The problem is Clark doesn't have a housekeeper. And when Syms asked the RCMP officer "for the name of his superior, she said he became "quite hostile" threatening to come to her office and trash it. "he said, "if you don't cooperate we can tear your place apart". Syms said "Somebody obviously thinks she has something they want."

That same week, Clark got a call from a long-time colleague at External Affairs who wanted to meet in an Ottawa swimming pool. Once there, Clark said the friend advised her to stay away from Glen Kealey, the Ottawa anti-corruption fighter who has helped publicize Clark's case. Kealey apparently was about to be "blown up" and if Clark didn't stay away from Kealey, she'd be "blown up" too.

AN OPEN LETTER
TO
JACK AUBRY, OTTAWA CITIZEN

October 30, 1998

To Fax No. : 613-232-2620

Dear Mr. Aubry:

Re: "Tory race turns bitter"
    October 27 article—Page A-3 (Saskatchewan farmer, David
    Orchard)

Are you aware that David Orchard is riding on a ticket that is a lie? I am certain that you will be interested in the enclosed document which came off the internet.

David Orchard and his associate Marjoleena Reepo have been attacking Shelley Ann Clark ever since she exposed the fraudulent FTA several years ago. I had the opportunity to meet her and asked her why she had not teamed up with David Orchard. Her response was direct. David Orchard had been approached by radio talk show hosts and many Canadians to appear with her in a public forum to debate the free trade issue. Orchard not only refused, but would not respond to phone calls or letters that asked him to do so.

Now I ask you Mr. Aubry, why Orchard, who claims to be vehemently opposed to the FTA, would flatly refuse the opportunity to team up with an eye witness to the misdeeds of the FTA. Put Orchard on the spot. Put the question to him publicly.

Is David Orchard "FOR" or "AGAINST" the FTA? Is his platform a complete and utter lie? Or is his EGO standing in the way of doing what is best for all fellow Canadians?

Sincerely,
A CARING CANADIAN

Chapter 20

The Mainstream Media "THE TRUTH"

The following article appeared in an American publication titled "THE JOURNALISTS" in July 1993 even though the author, John Swinton passed away in 1901, and what was stated back then stands true to this day.

The New York Times (December 16, 1901)

The article read "He was never afraid to speak what he believed boldly and unreservedly . . . It was his boast that he never, no matter what the ideas of his employers were, wrote a line contrary to his honest convictions as uttered on the stump . . . As a man of original ideas and freedom from the trammels of conventionality, Swinton had many admirers, even among those whose convictions were wholly opposed to his own".

John Swinton, the former Chief of Staff of the New York Times, called by his peers, "The Dean of his profession," was asked to give a toast before the New York Press Club. He responded with the following statement.

"There is no such thing, at this date of the world's history, in America, as an independent press. You know it and I know it. There is not one of you who dares to write your honest opinion, and if you did, you know beforehand that it would never appear in print. I am paid weekly to keep my honest opinion out of the paper I am connected with. Others of you are paid similar salaries for similar things, and any of you who would be so foolish as to write honest opinions would be out on the streets looking for another job. If I allowed my honest opinion to appear in one issue of my paper, before twenty-four hours my occupation would be gone. The business of the journalist is to destroy the truth; to lie outright; to pervert; to vilify; to fawn at the feet of mammon, and to sell his country . . . for his daily bread. You know it and I know it; and what folly is this toasting an independent press? <u>We are the tools and vassals for rich men behind the scenes</u>. We are the jumping jacks, they pull the strings and we dance. Our talents, our possibilities and our lives are all the property of other men. <u>We are intellectual prostitutes.</u>"

I would also like to bring to your attention an article that was written by Ottawa Journalist, Warren Kinsella that deals with the truth about the media.

Here are the views that he shared with his readers.

"Few things are as boring as the media writing about the media.

But unless you've been in a coma in the past couple of weeks, that's pretty much all you've been getting.

There's the British phone-hacking scandal which has toppled the News of the World and various luminaries within the Brit media-political establishment. That story may very well signal the end of Rupert Murdoch's media empire.

On this side of the pond, there have been nearly 200-200!—stories and columns written about Sun Media's determination to withdraw from the Ontario Press Council.

Many teeth have been gnashed, and many garments rent, over the Sun's decision. A goodly number of the disapproving comments, naturally, have come from the Sun's competitors.

Forgive me, dear reader, for being boring. But the piety has reached heretofore historic levels, and I can contain myself no longer."

Here, then, are Kinsella's Three Common Sense Observations about news media sins. Clip and save.

"Press councils and media ombudspersons are pretty useless.

If you have a serious beef about something that has been said about you, you have recourse: The civil law.

Press councils and ombudsmen, meanwhile, are inherently conflicted, as they get paid and/or are controlled by the very media organizations they are supposed to police.

An example: A few years back, I took now-deceased B.C. columnist (and Holocaust denier) Doug Collins to the B.C. Press Council for a series of errors and abuses. Throughout the process, I was left with the clear impression the B.C. body's principal interest was in running my complaint into the boards.

Their insistence that complainants give up their legal remedies in advance, in writing, suggested they were instruments to shield big media organizations from lawsuits.

The media is a special interest group
Politicians and Joe and Jane Frontporch know this already, but it amazes me how often some media bigwigs still don't. The media, to most of us, are simply big companies owned by other big companies. Like all big companies, they have biases aplenty.

So, when I penned a media column for the National Post, I was told I was not permitted to write anything positive about the CBC or the Toronto Star.

If I even quoted someone saying something remotely positive, it would end up on the Post's newsroom floor. (At the Sun, in case you are wondering, I have never been (a) told what to write, or (b) censored in any way, despite the fact that, as the resident Bolshevik, I periodically drive Brian Lilley, Mark Bonokoski and John Snobelen bonkers. Which upsets me a great deal, as you can imagine).

The media needs to take a pill

As in, take themselves way less seriously (as at the Sun, frankly). The technological revolution and the concurrent social media explosion has dramatically changed the rules of the game. Citizen media are now as important as the mainstream media.

To survive, the media companies need to be a lot more populist and a lot less po-faced. Nobody regards big media organizations as benign, impartial bodies anymore (if they ever did). They're just one of many voices competing for space on the public agenda. That's it.

There are more observations that could be made, but I want to avoid the greatest media sin of all. Which is, you know, being boring."

Chapter 21

Breakfast Meeting with the President of the Council of Canadians, Maude Barlow

To my surprise and amazement, the morning after my interview with CJOH TV's Charlie Greenwell had aired, I received a phone call at my home by none other than Ms. Maude Victoria Barlow, President of the Council of Canadians and author of several books. The one book that was of particular interest to me was "TAKE BACK THE NATION", published in 1992. I found the information quite valuable because it provided Canadians with a blue print on how to take back their country. Ms Barlow co-authored this book with Researcher, Bruce Campbell, who later played a valuable role as a witness to the discovery we made at Archives Canada. Maude invited me to meet with her for breakfast the next day at the Four Seasons Hotel. She wanted to hear more about my story and see if she could help.

After apprising Maude of the details of what I had witnessed at the Trade Negotiations Office, and the role that I played in the unfolding drama, she was mostly interested in the part that confirmed that Canadians had not been told or shown the "whole" Free Trade Agreement. The Agreement that had been agreed to, three minutes before the midnight deadline on October 3rd 1987. The Agreement that sold our country and forever changed the lives of Canadians. She was appalled at the possibility that most of the working papers had not reached Archives Canada, had been secretly transported to Germain Denis' car and that no one knew what he had done with them.

Maude wanted further proof that, in fact, these documents had not reached Archives Canada. In order to achieve this, she offered me the services of her co-author and researcher, Bruce Campbell. She said that Bruce and I should go together to the Archives Canada building and ask to see the Free Trade Documents. She felt certain that because I still had proof that I had worked at the Free Trade Negotiations Office, Bruce and I would be shown all the negotiating working papers as well as the deal itself.

Maude immediately contacted Bruce and set up a date and time for Bruce and I to meet in the lobby of the Library and Archives Canada building at 395 Wellington Street, right next door to the Parliament Buildings.

RENDEZ VOUS
AT
OTTAWA'S LIBRARY & ARCHIVES CANADA

I shall never forget that day. What we discovered was a shocker. After showing my Foreign Affairs ID, the Commissionaire gave us a pass to enter the building. The Commissionaire also told us that if we went directly to the receptionist, she would be able to tell us who we had to approach to view the Free Trade Negotiations' documents.

We were led to a huge room that looked like a stockroom. There was shelving from wall to wall and floor to ceiling. As we called out to make our presence known, a young man (I unfortunately do not recall his name) came out to ask how he could help us. We explained that we were looking for all the working papers for the free trade negotiations between Canada and the U.S. that had been sent to the archives. His response came as a surprise when he said oh! all of those papers dealing with the negotiations have been sent to another building just across the street. You will have to go there and ask.

Bruce and I thanked him and immediately proceeded to the building indicated. Upon entering the building, I felt a sense of secretiveness perhaps even surreal. It was a very old building and looked empty and austere with only one commissionaire on duty. We were once again sent up to an upper floor. When we arrived we were faced by double doors through which we entered without any security check.

A young man must have been forewarned of our imminent arrival as he quickly appeared to greet us. Once again, we explained what we were looking for. He told us to wait where we were, that he would be back in one minute. We were rather surprised at this because we knew that he could not possibly come up with all of the working papers we requested in that short period of time and by himself.

But as promised, he did re-appear in one minute holding one empty box. We were stunned. As we stared in disbelief, it took us a couple of minutes to recoup and ask the pertinent question. Where are all the free trade documents that were sent here to be catalogued and archived? You can imagine our shock when we were told that all free trade documents were in a bunker some 50 miles outside Ottawa. WHY? We both exclaimed at the very same moment. The young man replied "the Free Trade Agreement has been declared a matter of NATIONAL SECURITY".

It is very significant that after this incident at Archives Canada, I never heard from Bruce or Maude Barlow again. When I tried to reach her, she was never available and never returned my calls. This has puzzled me to this day. Maude Barlow, who had stood on Parliament Hill and been so vocal about the FTA being bad for Canadians, suddenly has an authentic eye witness who had seen the FTA in its entirety and had actually delivered it in person to Prime Minister Brian Mulroney. Yet, she chose to totally ignore this valuable asset who had been on the inside, behind the scenes for the entire negotiations; a person who had been one of the proof readers and was risking everything to warn Canadians about the fraud that had been perpetrated. This eyewitness would have supported Barlow's claims and helped her to convince Canadians to do something about it and not re-elect the perpetrators.

On August 6, 1993 an article appeared in the Ottawa Citizen on the issue of missing documents dealing with the cultural industry. The issue was that after nearly two years of delays, the Federal Government had finally responded to the Citizen's request for documents related to culture that had been negotiated in the Canada-U.S. free trade negotiations. THE GOVERNMENT HAD ONLY RELEASED 66 OF THE 1,400 PAGES IT IDENTIFIED AS RELEVANT TO THE REQUEST.

This author finds it incredible that the Ottawa Citizen and the Council of Canadians were solely concerned by the lack of documents dealing with our Canadian cultural industry. There is so much more information that Canadians are not being allowed to see; information on issues that will bring about serious difficulties in every area of their lives. Over the past 24 years, Canadians who have paid attention have seen the consequences of the Free Trade deal. The middle class and the poor in this country have a lot to worry about. Do Canadians not realize that the plan is to turn us into a society of "Kings and Serfs", thus completely eliminating the "middle class". What will it take for Canadians to wake up and step up to the plate and stop this travesty?

In 1993, when I ran in the Federal election, using the electoral process as a protective umbrella to speak to Canadians and let them know about the 'REAL FREE TRADE DEAL", I ran into another piece of evidence that confirmed the covert disappearance of key FTA documents. This evidence dealt with the department of Foreign Affairs (aka External Affairs) ordering Archives Canada personnel to tell anyone asking to see the Free Trade papers that the FTA had been declared "a matter of National Security." In my speeches, I kept mentioning the discovery that Bruce Campbell and I had made and that the documents for the Free Trade

Agreement could not be viewed by the public and was locked up in bunkers 50 miles outside Ottawa. These bunkers were named after former Prime Minister John Diefenbaker. The Diefenbaker bunkers eventually became a tourist attraction. Where are the Free Trade Negotiations working papers today?

It is significant, that after delivering several of these speeches to the constituents in my riding, my campaign manager, John Bowlby, brought to my attention an advertisement that appeared in the Ottawa Citizen. This article invited all Canadians to come and view the Free Trade Agreement in the main lobby of the Library and Archives Canada building.

John and I immediately rushed over to see if this invitation was genuine. Unfortunately, when we arrived in the lobby we were not surprised at what we saw. Was this a hoax? How insulting—did they believe that Canadians are brain dead? Here is a description of what we saw in the main lobby. In the middle of the room, standing by itself, was a glass case under lock and key. Inside the case, leaning against a prop, was the cover page of the "Canada-U.S. Free Trade Agreement". THAT WAS IT. That is what the government was allowing Canadians to be privy to.

This begs the question: "WHAT ARE THEY HIDING FROM YOU?

Chapter 22

Letter to Preston Manning, Leader, Reform Party

The following is a precise replica of the original letter from Preston Manning's Office Manager, Valerie Clark. It has been re-typed for the sole purpose of incorporating it onto the pages of this chapter.

02/15/94   403-238-3855   PAGE 01

Dear Preston,

I had a discussion recently with Harry about Shelley-Anne Clarke, the woman who claims that during her employment with the Mulroney Government, she had some upper-level dealings with the paperwork regarding NAFTA.* She has now gone public, as I am sure you are aware, with information regarding some alleged improprieties in this regard.

When I spoke to Harry, he indicated that the feeling in your office was that, without any substantiating evidence, Ms. Clarke's allegations were unfounded.

Ms. Clarke has explained very clearly why she was unable to come away from the situation with written information to back up her claims. She is bringing forward claims that information exists that could have extremely serious ramifications in Canada with regard to its trade dealings with the United States. She asks only that this issue be investigated, and cites many reasons why there is good and just cause to seek out and examine the paperwork in question.

The following note contained within the parenthesis is not part of Valerie Clark's letter. It is a clarification of which trade agreement the author is dealing with.

{Valerie Clark is referring to the wrong agreement. I was dealing with the Canada-U.S.A. Free Trade Agreement, the FTA not NAFTA, the North American Free Trade Agreement that involved Mexico.}

My feeling is that we have no proof that Ms. Clarke has lacked integrity or been dishonest in the past. Here is a woman who loves and has served her country well, voicing, at great risk to herself, some concerns over the handling of the trade negotiations. I feel it is incumbent upon those who are in power in the Government to now order that the archives be opened and the documentation in question scrutinized. After all, what could Ms. Clarke have to gain by lying? And what does Canada have to lose if she is, in fact, telling the truth?

If the paperwork is brought out from the archives where it is purportedly being stored, and examined by experts in trade law, then the matter can be put to rest as to whether or not Ms. Clarke's allegations are true and her concerns well-founded.

As your constituent, I would ask that you please request the disinterment of these documents so that they may be examined to ascertain the validity of Ms. Clarke's allegations.

Yours truly,

Valerie Clark
Cc: Reform Party of Canada, Ottawa

Valerie Clark
31 Canova Road W.
Calgary, Alberta, Canada
T2W 4B3

Telephone: (403) 238-4675
FAX: (403) 238-3855

N.B.: I was never contacted by anyone from Preston Manning's Office. A group of Canadians who were assisting me did a follow-up with his office. No one responded.

Chapter 23

Meeting/Royal Canadian Mounted Police (1993)

My recollection of the meeting is as follows:

Reform Party Member of Parliament, Jack Ramsay of Alberta, was the one man with the integrity and the bravery to bring my explosive disclosure on the Canada-U.S. Free Trade Agreement to the attention of the entire House of Commons. Jack Ramsay, a former RCMP officer, had the courage to insist that my allegations be investigated.

Jack Ramsay arranged for me to meet with the RCMP in the safe sanctuary of his Parliament Hill Office. In attendance at this meeting were several supporters: Charles Frey, John Bowlby, John Goodfellow and Jack Ramsay. Two senior RCMP officers from the Criminal Investigations Unit represented the RCMP.

The meeting was short-lived as one of the RCMP officers opened up a file he had in his hands. The file consisted of one letter that reportedly came from an MP who had reported a sexual harassment complaint on one Shelley Ann Clark.

When Jack Ramsay realized what was happening he immediately intervened and advised the RCMP that we were not there on a sexual harassment complaint, but on a more serious matter—the fraudulent Canada-U.S. Free Trade Agreement; that he had documents provided to him by Shelley Ann Clark that clearly demonstrated that fraudulent acts had been committed by the Mulroney government with regard to this Agreement.

When Jack Ramsay insisted that they take the documents that he was offering, the RCMP officer immediately shut the file he had just opened, refused to accept the documents that Ramsay had offered and then advised us that: "this meeting is over" and they walked out.

One of the witnesses, Mr. Charles Frey, has sent me his recollection of that meeting and I pass it on to you to ensure that you are apprised of all aspects that took place.

Mr. Frey states: "Shelley Ann had ample reason to ask John Bowlby, John Goodfellow and myself to accompany her to a meeting with two very senior RCMP officers, to whom she disclosed the perfidious, sycophantic actions by our elected representatives, implemented in the overriding interest of an international, self-appointed elite, (which readily admits targeting/ co-opting/assisting them on their path to power).

This meeting took place in the generous Parliament Hill offices of Mr. Ramsay, MP, the Reform Party's Justice Critic; a retired RCMP officer himself.

Mr. Ramsay informally officiated over this embarrassing encounter until he was informed by his secretary, at about mid-point, that his presence was required on the Floor for an impending vote.

Overcome by impatience, engendered by their abject lack of indication of any life, I asked the RCMP investigators whether it was their opinion that no crime was committed by lying to the Premiers of Canada, since they were not signatories to the federal-managed FTA.

They nodded and muttered agreement."

Chapter 24

Media or Spin Doctors?

SHELLEY ANN CLARK
NATIONAL PARTY OF CANADA
CAMPAIGN HQ

October 25, 1993

OPEN LETTER TO THE EDITOR

THE MANOTICK MESSENGER

FAX NO: 692-3758

Dear Sir,

RE: YOUR ARTICLE "FREE TRADE QUESTION—
NOT ISSUE OF OCTOBER 20, 1993

What an incredible tale you spin. This information is to all Canadians; our country is threatened by political takeover. Instead of helping Canada remain intact, all you can think of is slander. At least you could have been accurate.

Your article implies that this story is a fabrication "by someone who watches too much afternoon TV". For the record, I rarely watch T.V. I have been very busy for many months with volunteer work between Ottawa and Cornwall.

The statement by Therese McKellar "that it's just National Party propaganda" is unwarranted; she did not participate in the Free Trade Negotiations. According to her own statement "I am a chartered accountant and have a business with my husband". This Sir, tells me that she has not been working in any Government office and she certainly does not have sufficient facts. She is obviously grasping at straws to save her crumbling party.

THESE ARE THE FACTS:

- On May 26, 1993, long before this election was announced, a disclosure was made by my lawyer to the Prime Minister of Canada, the Opposition leaders, the 10 provincial premiers and the main stream media. Someone paid attention.

- Charlie Greenwell, Insider's Report, CJOH-TV, did his own investigation to the satisfaction of CJOH lawyers. This story was broadcasted June 3, 1993.

With regard to Mr. Bellemare's offer to meet with the Auditor General. You report "Clark did not say if she would accept the offer". Once again you erred.

A) I did accept Mr. Bellemare's offer in French, at the microphone in front of the Manotick audience;

B) According to your article you mention that Mr. Bellemare offered that he and I meet with the Auditor General. This puzzles me, for the Auditor General had nothing to do with the Free Trade Agreement.

C) On October 21, 1993 at the All Candidates meeting in Metcalfe, Mr. Bellemare stated to the audience that he had already made arragements for me to meet with Lloyd Axworthy, Liberal Trade Critic, after the election and that I had agreed to do so.

With regard to the statement on Tom Hockin. Mr. Hockin was not the Deputy Minister for International Trade during the Free Trade Negotiations nor was he part of the team that put together the final text. *Gerald E. Shannon was the Deputy Minister.* By the time Mr. Hockin was on the scene all documents used in the negotiations had been removed from the Trade Negotiations Office.

With regard to Michael Wilson's spokesperson I am certain that he was shocked when he received your call. He certainly was never at the Trade Negotiations Office midnight sessions when Germain Denis and I were there alone altering these document. I previously stated this in a report to the Public Service Alliance dated July 1988, the May 26, 1993 disclosure, the CJOH broadcast of June 3rd '93 and again to the Montreal Mirror on August 19th '93.

I am sure your readers and everyone else residing in Carleton-Gloucester would like to know what induced you to publish such an inaccurate piece of journalism. I WAS THERE—I should know. I AM PROUD TO BE A CANADIAN AND I WISH TO REMAIN ONE.

Sincerely,

S. A. Clark

Shelley Ann Clark

c.c.: Tri-Valley Crier
Carleton Review
Mr. Eugene Bellemare, Liberal M.P.

Chapter 25

Letter to the Hon. Roy MacLaren, Minister for International Trade (1994)

April 26, 1994

Hon. Roy MacLaren
Minister for International Trade
Ottawa, Ontario
K1A 0G2

FAX # (613) 996-8924

Dear Minister,

CANADA/U.S. FREE TRADE AGREEMENT

My name is Shelley Ann Clark. I am an employee of the Department of Foreign Affairs. During 1986-88 I was employed as Executive Assistant to Mr. Germain Denis, the present serving Assistant Deputy Minister for Multilateral Trade. Mr. Denis, in 1986-88, was the third ranking negotiator at the Trade Negotiations Office (TNO), under Ambassadors Simon Reisman and Gordon Ritchie. While at TNO, I was ordered by Mr. Denis to doctor the Briefing Books which were used to mislead the Provincial Premiers about the impact on their Province as a result of Canada-USA Free Trade Negotiations (FTA).

Minister, each statement I have heard you make in reply to the allegations made by me leads me to believe that you have been misinformed about the facts concerning this matter. <u>FOR THE RECORD</u> please allow me to mention some specific examples:

TO—Diane Ablonczy, Reform Party M.P. (Calgary) on January 20, 1994 in response to a question asked in the House of Commons you stated "the allegations made by the Shelley Ann Clark were investigated by the previous Government and found to be unwarranted."

COMMENT—This statement is untrue. At my request an interview was conducted at my home by ONE RCMP officer. I was told by this officer, Inspector Pierre Droz, that this was strictly an interview in order to determine whether the RCMP <u>should</u> conduct an investigation. Later this same officer notified me that they arrived at the decision that there would be <u>NO</u> investigation due to the following reasons: 1) I had no documents to prove that what I was saying was true; and 2) THE RCMP SAW NO MOTIVE since the Prime Minister did not require the signature of the Premiers in order to pass the Free Trade Agreement.

TO—Diane Ablonczy, Reform Party M.P. (Calgary) on January 20, 1994 in the House of Commons you stated "the text made available by the previous government is, IN MY UNDERSTANDING, the actual text."

COMMENT—With all due respect Mr. Minister, can you please explain since when do independent investigators accept denials made by the perpetrators of a crime, as solid proof of its non-occurrence? "Canadians have not seen the complete text."

Furthermore, if one needed more reason to doubt the veracity of the responses made by the Commissioners of the Royal Canadian Mounted Police, one need only examine the numerous adamant denials made about the existence of political interference, as affirmed by Norman Inkster, RCMP Commissioner, when he first appeared before the Standing

Committee of the House of Commons on Justice and the Solicitor General, on June 1 and 13, 1989. Inkster's first knee-jerk denials should be viewed only in the light of his later apologies, on November 21 and December 12, 1989, when he finally admitted to "having misled the Committee".

Also, one remembers that on July 16, 1991 the top RCMP brass, three Commissioners, were each charged by senior Justice of the Peace Lynn Coulter with "ceasing and limiting many police investigations". Obviously, only back-room political manoeuvres, not <u>evidence presented in an open and public courtroom</u>, allowed the allegedly corrupt RCMP brass to escape these serious criminal charges totally unscathed.

TO—Jack Ramsay, Reform Party M.P. (Edmonton) in a private conversation he reportedly shared with you, and later relayed back to me. I quote Mr. Ramsay, quoting you Mr. Minister, "It's old news. It's water under the bridge."

COMMENT—The implications of what I witnessed (see attached gist of my declarations) are expected to have far reaching implications on the political independence of Canada. In my view, and by reading incoming correspondence, (the number of Canadians writing to the Institute has seen an enormous increase in the past few months) by caring Canadians who write to the Institute I would have to say "it would never be too late for true patriots to act in support of their country."

TO—David Kilgour, Liberal Party M.P. (Edmonton).
In your letter of April 15, 1994 responding to his enquiry of March 16, 1994 you stated "I can assure you that these allegations have been carefully investigated and that the 'appropriate authorities' have found no substance to them".

COMMENT—I repeat, who investigated these allegations? Why was I not notified of this supposed investigation which supposedly took place. Why was I not contacted for questioning? Why were Germain Denis and I not offered the opportunity to submit to a proper polygraph (lie detector)? As well, to whom do you refer Mr. Minister when you stated to Mr. Kilgour "the appropriate authorities have found no substance to them (my allegations)? Who are these mysterious people who know so much, without ever having received any evidence to base their conclusions on? Minister, who else in your view, but the entire Canadian public are capable, ultimately, of passing judgement on the veracity of my public allegations about this serious matter, where I alleged high treason on the part of two very important, politically protected, government officials (one who has been relocated recently by the department, to a work space adjoining my own)?

Mr. Minister, in a letter received yesterday April 25, 1994 from my Liberal Member of Parliament (Carleton-Gloucester) Eugene Bellemare, I am informed that a certain Mr. Michael Conway, a senior official of the Department of Foreign Affairs has been assigned to my case. It seems strange to me at least, because this letter was apparently typed on March 28, 1994 a full month ago. To date, I have not been contacted by Mr. Conway. I can state, however, that everything imaginable has been attempted by the Department of Foreign Affairs since Mr. Conway's appointment, to create as many difficulties for me as possible and to make my life insufferable.

First, an insurance claim for loss or damage done to my personal effects (relocation Geneva-Ottawa ordered by DFAIT) was grabbed by the Department of Foreign Affairs and applied to some unspecified medical debt purportedly having been incurred, while I was on service for my country, abroad.

Second, my take-home pay was cut in half (from $1,000 to $500) reportedly for the same reason—even though Treasury Board Policy/Regulations clearly state deductions should be limited to 10% of the net income of each individual on a per pay basis. With the kind of help I am apparently being provided with behind the scenes by Mr. Conway, one needs no enemies.

These actions left me with no alternative but to declare immediate personal bankruptcy. The fall-out of that event saw the Royal Bank (located in the Pearson building) close my account; but not before helping themselves to the other half of my pay, in order to satisfy their claim. The Royal Bank proceeded to dishonour all my outstanding cheques, including the pre-authorised payments of my car insurance, food merchant and Cable TV. They have also since refused to return these NSF cheques to my creditors, thus making redemption impossible, thereby aggravating credit problems.

Mr. Minister, I accept all that is being done to me in the spirit of one who cares for my country, however, I do not wish to have it said later that you were not personally aware of the specifics of my declarations. It is with this in mind that I would like to take this opportunity to repeat the information I disclosed to my union, the Public Service Alliance of Canada, (PSAC) in July 1988; to the Premiers, with the assistance of a lawyer in a letter dated May 26, 1993; to Charlie Greenwell, INSIDER'S REPORT on CJOH Television in June 1993; and lastly, communicated to all Liberal Ministers, in a letter dated December 1993.

Because no one in positions of power will investigate this important matter, I am left with no other alternative but to accept the numerous invitations coming my way, to speak publicly at conferences and on open-line radio shows heard on air both here and abroad.

Here again is the gist of my "OLD NEWS"—

— The Trade Negotiations Office GEAC computer system was compromised from the start. All secret files could be accessed by phone—some in fact were.

— Germain Denis, the third ranking negotiator and not Simon Reisman was the true and only BOSS at TNO. Only he would approve our final position papers that would go into the briefing books. Contrary to the normal chain of command he was in regular telephone contact with Prime Minister Brian Mulroney.

— Denis followed written instructions as laid down for him in THE IMPLEMENTATION SCHEME. I saw the SCHEME while packing boxes to take to his car. It directed him to give away control over Canada's natural resources, including our ENERGY, WATER, MINERALS and AGRICULTURE, as well as to HARMONIZE Canada's SOCIAL PROGRAMS with those of the USA. It spoke of Lucien Bouchard, Quebec's separation by 1995 and the construction of Simon Riesman's GRAND CANAL water diversion project at James Bay—all done in final preparation for the eventual total political assimilation of Canada by the USA, by the year 2005.

— Denis DOCTORED the Premier's Briefing Books and personally lied to them during oral briefings. He also ordered the shredding of numerous documents at night and stole document which made up the doctored version of the Premier's briefing books in lieu of sending them to our archives as ordered by TNO ADMINISTRATIVE MEMO dated March 1988. (as specified in my report to PSAC dated July 22, 1988)

As one passionately proud Canadian I cannot, and will not, stand by while our country presently known as CANADA is bartered away by traitors.

Sincerely,

S. A. Clark

Shelley Ann Clark

cc: Diane Ablonczy, MP
Jack Ramsey, MP
David Kilgour, MP
Eugene Bellemare, MP
Michael Conway, Act. Director General Personnel Administration
Lloyd Fucile, Executive Secretary, National Component, PSAC.

ALL MINISTERS
ALL MEMBERS OF PARLIAMENT
ALL CANADIANS

Chapter 26

INTERROGATION by the RCMP
(June 23,1993)

June 23, 1993 was to be my first day on the campaign trail as a candidate in the Federal elections for Mel Hurtig's National Party. Imagine my surprise when at 8:00 a.m. as I was preparing to go out the door to meet with my campaign manager, John Bowlby I received a phone call from Inspector Pierre Droz of the Major Fraud Investigation Unit of the Royal Canadian Mounted Police (RCMP). I was not asked, but I was told to stay put that they would be coming to my home at 10:00 a.m. as they had to interview me before I could hit the campaign trail. I immediately contacted my agent, my campaign manager and my lawyer to ask them to be at this interview (aka interrogation) so that they could be witnesses. The following 41 pages tells all. The Conservative government in power at that time and the Liberals who won that election could never say that "they" did not know that our country had been sold and that they knew nothing about all the "irregular" activities that took place in the Canadian Free Trade Negotiations Office. The RCMP had all the information and so did the Liberal Minister for International Trade, the Honorable Roy MacLaren (Ref my letter to MacLaren under Chapter 25).

TRANSCRIPT

RCMP INTERVIEW

DATE: JUNE 23, 1993

PRESENT: Inspector Pierre Droz, Major Fraud Investigation Unit, Harold C. Funk, Lawyer, Marguerite Bowlby, CABL (Citizens Against Bad Law) Member of the Executive and Shelley Ann Clark

Introduction: John Richard Bowlby, CABL Member of the Executive

Location: Residence of Shelley Ann Clark

N.B.   For purposes of clarification, any corrections or additions to this transcript is identified by the presence of brackets. The dotted lines mean that I could not make out what the person was saying.

              For purposes of identification of the individuals present Inspector Droz=I, Harold Funk=H, Marguerite Bowlby=M, John Richard Bowlby=J and Shelley Ann Clark=S.

J: This recording was made Wednesday, June the 23rd, 1993 at approximately—starting at approximately 10:10 in the morning at 59 Winnegreen Crescent (Court), Ottawa, Ontario.

H: How long have you been with the force?

I: . . . .

H: Whenever you want to start I'll put on the tape and I'll give you the people here Pierre Droz and he's an Inspector of the Major Fraud Unit of the RCMP, Marg Bowlby is here and my client is here . . . I would say cooperate with the RCMP in this matter and answer any questions that you might have with regard . . . .

I: . . . What I'm here for is the fact that you had some instructions to change something on a document so I want you to from the start to tell me how it happened and why and who knows about it.

S: OK. The—I did not change a document. I'll start from the beginning—that beginning January '87 one Mr. Germain Denis was appointed and parachuted into the position of Assistant Chief Negotiator for the Free Trade Negotiations. When they (Simon Reisman and his team) would go I was put in charge of preparing the briefing books and supervising their preparation for the main trade negotiations that went on in Washington with the federal—with our federal people, Simon Reisman, Ambassador Gordon Ritchie and the team that would travel with them to Washington. Now, shortly after that the discussions

H: How many people did you have on staff under you to prepare these books.

S: Oh I would have a team that—of 15-20 people that was helping me. I remember one time 35. It varied depending on how much material had to be put together, but I had—but these were the federal books. What I want to point out now is that when we started briefing the provinces I was suddenly told that No I could not get any help with the provincial books so that immediately—I am highly trained with security having been with External Affairs all of my life so that it peaked my curiosity immediately as to why can't I get help when there are 10 provinces to deal with. Then I was asked also to—that when it came to dealing with the briefing books for the provinces I had to have some kind of mark that was not visible to anyone to keep the provincial books completely separate from the federal ones and I understood that a little later when I received my first phone call from—I was married at the time—the phone call came through about 10:30 at night for me to meet with Germain Denis at 11:00 p.m. because he had something to do. what

I: We're talking about '87.

S: Yes. We were talking

I: What month of '87?

S: This all began in January '87.

I: OK.

S: Now when I arrived there they had of course come back from a negotiating session in Washington and I was told to take apart the federal briefing book very carefully so that I would know how to put it back together again without anyone knowing that it had been taken apart and certain—all the areas that Germain Denis was responsible for 4/5 major areas of the negotiations and it was his 4/5 areas of the negotiations that was pulled out and I was told to bring each area up on the screen and as I brought them up on the screen Germain Denis would carefully go over the federal book and I would be told that for the provincial book that the one I would pull out of the printer would be for the provincial book and make sure not to mix it up with the other one (the federal briefing book) and entire paragraphs were deleted—sometimes it was just a line sometimes it was a paragraph and figures were altered. At first I thought Ok its because they've just negotiated and there have been—you know when you're negotiating things are changing all the time so I thought that we were going to do the same to the federal book to keep the federal book updated but when I presented that that well 'am I to do the federal book now?' he (Denis) said NO we do not—the federal book remains as is—we don't touch it. So this same scene repeated itself throughout the entire negotiations right up til October 3rd, 1987 when it was signed in Washington.

I: That—that would not be '87 that would be

S: No. No. It was signed on October 3rd, 1987. The version that was tabled in the House. Because we were shutting down by March 1988 we were shutting down—we were shutting down and it's all documented in the document that you provided to the RCMP, Harry. That March 1988 was when the shut down began.

H: So this began in January of 1987 then.

S: Yes. Because 1986

H: The meetings (briefings) with the provinces.

S: Yes. Exactly. Because before then Germain Denis was Multilateral Trade. He was not doing the Free Trade Ok. So that's why I begin with the Free Trade January—December-January. Because I remember you see, the Uruguay Round took place in the fall of '86 so I know we were not involved—I was not involved with the Free Trade in the Fall of '86. I was there physically in the Trade Negotiations Office, but it was during that fall that the leak came out in the newspaper accusing the Prime Minister of having hired only anglophones in the senior positions for the negotiations and all of a sudden Germain Denis was taken away from Multilateral Trade which he had been doing for years and parachuted in to the Senior Assistant Chief Negotiator position. So that's when the involvement began with Germain Denis. And I was . . . —everytime—I dont think you have a copy of the relevant papers of the appointment book because I checked the appointment book that I kept all of Germain Denis' appointments during that period of time. In my appointment book it shows every time there was a Washington main negotiation and approximately a week later you see that there was a provincial briefing. And, on other occasions you see that there was a one on one meeting with the provinces. Now every time, about 48 hours prior to the provincial briefings we would know when they were coming because we were the ones inviting them. I would be called at home around 11:00 o'clock at night—brought in for midnight and I would be there until four in the morning making these changes and it was the specific instructions, you know, that really alerted me that what I was doing was illicit. And, because the instructions were so specific—as to my being extremely—you know there could be no mistake that I would hand over a federal briefing book instead of a provincial one. The provinces—after I would put together the books until four in the morning they would be the ones that were locked up in his vault while the others were allowed to be out in my area in an ordinary cabinet with just the bar not the vault it was just the cabinet with the bar that—they would be locked up. The provinces were complaining and they complained directly to the Prime Minister's Office and nothing was done about it. That they were receiving—I was ordered to give them the books only after they were seated at the table. They were suppose to get the books at least two hours before to be able to go through the briefing book to—you know, to look at what was happening. They were not given that chance. I was under strict orders that the books were never to be released beforehand. The books had to be brought in to them once they were already seated. So, they complained to the Prime Minister bitterly. The Prime Minister's Office called me knowing that I was the person in charge of these books. They put all the blame on me. And I was told 'to shut up—to put up with the blame' because I said 'its not me' and everybody in TNO (Trade Negotiations Office) knew it wasn't me but the delays were caused by Germain Denis. Because you take

Alan Nymark who was representing Federal-Provincial Relations was having a fit. He (Alan Nymark) was working next door to us and he and his assistant knew that Germain Denis was causing the delay and they were absolutely furious. There was an ongoing battle about that. Then I would be—I would have to number. I would have to keep a list: Book No. 1, this province had it. Manitoba had it; Book No. 2, Saskatchewan had it. So and so on.

I: Uhm Uhm

S: So that if one book was not returned I would know which province would (did) not return it. Then I was ordered that after the books were brought back to me I would go in again during the middle of the night to destroy—I had to destroy nine out of the ten books, but I had to keep one complete book. Take it out of the binder because it took up too much room in his cabinet

I: Uhm Uhm

S: and to keep that one complete book each time, a copy of it in his (Denis) cabinet because you see each time he made the alterations he had to know what he had said the previous time. So by keeping one copy each time, when I would be called in the following—to working during the night the following time he (Denis) would go in to his cabinet and retrieve what he had said to them the previous time and go by those notes to make the alternations.

I: Uh Uh

S: After doing it for I guess—by the first time I did it and I saw to the degree the stuff was being altered but not altered in the fed books—I began to be extremely scared for myself because I said 'this is illicit—I'm collaborating in this even though it's under instruction and under threat' because I was always under threat.

I: What told you it was (was) illicit?

S: What told me it was illicit.

I: The purpose could be real. I mean that's that's the truth—that that has to be put in the book.

S: No, because what

I: What tells (told) you it was wrong? To do that.

S: What was wrong. A lot of things told me it was wrong. Why was he making me do it in the middle of the night? I was the only one in there in the middle of the night

I: It does not mean . . . intent because they're doing it at night.

S: No, but also why were the figures in the federal book different than the provincial books and why was I never. We were—Why were we not using

I: After, after all the negotiations were done, if a province want to refer to the federal book—they could, I guess.

S: No they couldn't. They were sent—the federal books were all collected. My memo (TNO Admin Memo) in my documentation shows that we received a Memo to submit all federal negotiating books.

I: Well it's public. I don't think they they can

S: No, but now the version that's public—what I'm trying to make you understand is the version that is public is the legal version and the legal language and once. Once the Prime Minister

I: Well, is that the official one?

S: . . . The one that was given to the Archives

I: The official one. The one it should be referred to if there is a a a—any problem or anything

S: But why why

I: between the United States and Canada, I think the one who should refer to. It's the one (Inspector Droz laughs)

S: But the provinces didn't want to go along with, with the deal, and they

H: May I ask you a question?

S: Yes.

H: The Federal Briefing Books—they would have changed over these proceedings over a period of time with the negotiations with the United States?

S: Yes.

H: Ok. And those briefing books were changed because of negotiations and you would make those changes or your staff would?

S.   Yes. The various people . . . .

H: When these briefing books. The final briefing books Ok.

S: Yes.

H: Were they—that went in to the Archives. Were those briefing books be a series of briefing books or only one briefing book. That were finally put in to the Archives whey they were requested.

S: What was finally put in to the Archives was uh. The memo requested that all the material that had been used in the negotiations

I: Uhm Uhm

S: be given to the person in charge of cataloging for the Archives.

H: What what material did you provide to them then? For that . . . .

S: None.

H: For the

S: Because Germain—for the, for the

H: For the federal briefing books

S: For the federal briefing books Germain Denis uh just said 'his men (would) look after it, but the provincial books

H: No. I'm just asking about the federal

S: Ok. The federal books—the federal books uh . . . he was responsible for the federal books and what I had out in my area was given.

H: Can you tell us exactly what was given to the Archives?

S: Well, I can't—you know. All I know it was his areas: government procurement, intellectual property uh agriculture, government procurement, agriculture, tariffs, subsidies and intellectual property. Now those were the Germain Denis areas that he was responsible for and the federal—I had a section that said FEDERAL-PROVINCIAL

BOOKS and all of the negotiating documents that had been put into the federal book—I kept a copy out in my area. He kept a copy of the other stuff in his vaulted cabinet so then all material (that) was requested to be given to the Archives. Whatever was used in the negotiations it was—whatever material was used for the negotiations 'you are to provide so and so of the Archives with all the material. Now two hours after that memo arrived at his (Denis) desk he came in—saw it—pulled me in to his office and said 'we have to move quick (quickly)—sit down—I'll explain my instructions to you and I was told you know 'you tell anybody this and I'm going to see to it that you never work in Ottawa again as long as you live. You will be finished with government' and that's when he gave me the instructions that all the provincial material that he had been keeping in his, in his vault. They had to be taken to his car.

I: Ok.

S: And he (Denis) said the way we're going to do it and he gave me the list of procedures. He said 'the way you're going to do it if you're going to do it at one hour intervals but if you're finding out that people are getting suspicious you're going to move it to two hour intervals and you're going to put the stuff in Xerox boxes. He then handed me his car keys.

I: Uh Uh

S: I refused to do it.

I: . . . take time

S: Oh yes. Ok. Everything is there that—the procedure that I had to follow. Uh He also had advised me—I was asking him what he (Denis) was doing with all his classified material (used in the negotiations)—because there was

146

a procedure (for material used in the negotiations) within the Trade Negotiations Office with the Head of Security, Guy Marcoux—that you could not go and destroy (material used in the negotiations) something yourself. Anything that would be destroyed would have to have an authorization and Guy Marcoux would look after bringing it to the Pearson building for proper destruction. Now he didn't—he (Denis) could not follow that order. He could not do that. That's why he had me sneak them out in Xerox boxes.

I: Uh Uh

S: Because the person that would have to sign, agreeing that they could be destroyed so that they didn't reach the Archives—because he (Denis) said "these cannot reach the Archives". The person would have had to read the material and they would have said well why, why are we stuck with two sets of, two sets of negotiations. So that's what it boiled down to. They had to appease the provinces and he told me. He said we have—they were having—the provinces were giving them a hell of a hard time if you remember. They (the provinces) didn't want to go along with uh any of it and they were given them a rough time and to appease the provinces they were giving them this wrong information. They were altering the information to appease the provinces.

H: Can I ask a question? You may not want to answer it—the question. But if I was to make a Freedom of Information application to the government to see the briefing books of the provinces uh would those briefing books be available to me? You must know that by now whether those briefing books are available and are part of the documentation. Because the provinces had those briefing books in front of them and they were obviously briefed on those books and they obviously made notes on those books and all I'm saying is if her story is true/is false if in fact the briefing books are available and if the provinces have a right to see those books and I would submit that they have a right to and if her story is true then those briefing books would not be available to me or they wouldn't be available to you?

S: They would be non-existent.

I: Cough Cough

H: Are they available to you (Inspector Droz) is the question—that I would like to ask you. Are those books there? Can you advise me?

I: Sure. Ok.

S: Because what I am telling you is what

H: Excuse me. I just want to ask one other question. I think it's an important question because I—I would like you to also check with the provinces if whatever, Ontario I guess is the easiest one, as to whether the provinces have any notes from their officials with regard to the briefings? Because with those notes that they have you will be able to check it very carefully with the briefing books of the federal government.

I: Sure. I think uh, I'm sure they read their book after the, the uh I'm sure they compare their notes with the book they received and would complain after. That's that's what bugs me. Uh I'm sure if you go to a lawyer or a notary—and you sign something uh when you receive the deed—when you receive the deed one week after you reread the deed and make sure it's what you say, what you signed.

S: They (the provinces) were not allowed to bring the briefing books back with them though.

I: . . . .

S: I had to collect the briefing books—I had to collect the briefing books and pull them apart—destroy nine of them and keep that that one copy.

I: I'm sure they took notes. They they

S: They must have taken notes on their . . . .

I: Sure. They came up with some documentation too, the provinces. I'm sure.

H: Is there any way . . . .

I: It's impossible.

H: Ok. Could they

I: I'm sure that they didn't only rely on the government, on the federal government for the Free Trade Agreement . . . .

H: . . . .

I: And uh

S: I'm sure they had their own ideas.

I: So uh they—surely they came up with something. And uh they have photocopies of notes or anything. I'm sure that after they received their copy that they went through and I'm sure they compared their notes with the final

H: They didn't get a copy of the Free Trade—the briefing book.

S: No. No.

H: They didn't get a copy. If you want to ask the provinces whether they got a copy of the briefing book.

I: I will. I will.

H: Because they didn't get a copy of the briefing book. They were all taken back from them. Ok

S: That's why I had them numbered. One, I was told I had to numbered them.

I: . . . A book telling them what the negotiations were and what they reached. I'm sure they have something. It's almost impossible.

H: To prevent them . . . .

S: They would have had to

H/I: . . . .

S: They would have had to take notes because their books—I know I had to collect them back, because if there would have been one book missing.

I: It's not a secret book. It's a public book.

S: The federal one is a public book.

I: And only the final version is the real one. So what happened before the final version that's. I would have to look at . . . .

H: Briefing books—Provincial briefing books that were given. The provinces were brought in at 9 o'clock in the morning.

I: Uh Uh

H: They stayed until 5 o'clock in the afternoon.

I: Uh Uh

H: The saw the briefing books given by Mr. Denis that been changed from the federal to the provincial to brief them. At the end of the meeting those books were taken away. The officers for the provinces would have made notes on the sections that they were never given a copy of that briefing book that they could check. they would come in another time to be briefed and they were never given a copy of that book to check with. What I'm asking you—the notes will only make sense to the people that were there if they—if there is a briefing book that relates to what in fact was there. It's not there any more.

I: Let let's say the, the provinces were to meeting with . . . so they wrote down some notes, and the next book what the the what they were talking about in the first meeting is different in the next book they received. They would have complained I'm sure.

H: No. Because

S: No because it was altered each time.

H: Altered each time.

S: Each time. That's we're trying to tell you. For a whole year I went in there you know, at those hours to

I: Well I'm sure . . . .

S: It's all written down in my appointment book each time they came and the forty-eight hours before I would be brought in. I was told . . . .

I: That, I understand, but the final version. I'm sure they read it.

S: Now, what you don't understand

H: The final brief was burned

S: The final version

H: (laughter)

S: I was there right through to the end—right through to the closure and I was one of the major seven proof readers. There was seven of us proof reading THE VERSION meaning the federal version.

I: Uh. Uh.

S: And I remember that I'm the one because of my . . . that was able to pick up on several areas and brought it to an honest Konrad VonFinckenstein. He was the head in charge of the legal language for the book. Konrad had 4/5 lawyers working in there with him on the book.

I: Uh Uh

S: And, and the thing that I picked up on because I couldn't remember everything—there was too much—that some of the major changes that had been made, I remembered and when I read the federal—when I was proofing that federal version I went to the head lawyer, Konrad VonFinckenstein and I said 'Konrad this is not right'

I: What did he say?

S: And he said 'holy shiet thank God you caught that because he said you're right, I (Konrad) was there at the—in Washington and I (Shelley Ann) was dead right. I was dead right and Konrad—the few that I was able to catch, Konrad VonFinckenstein fixed. And he got it fixed immediately. I mean, he pulled in several lawyers in minutes and it was fixed right there in front of me.

H: I want to ask another question.

I: Ok. Can I get in touch with this gentleman?

S: Konrad VonFinckenstein is now an ADM (Assistant Deputy Minister) in the Department of Justice and he will remember me very well because he couldn't believe the stuff I was bringing to him and that I would write.

H: Can you . . . .

I: Sorry. Do you . . . .

S: Yes. The Department of Justice right here on Wellington Street.

I: How do you spell his name.

S: Von is right Finckenstein is F I C K E N S T E I N.

I: . . . .

S: Now Konrad would remember.

I: Ok. I just . . . .

H: Now you've advised the officer

S: I didn't tell him why I had the information because I was under threat not to tell.

H: You advised this gentleman about the contact between Germain Denis and the Prime Minister over a period of time.

S: Yes. You see that, that was not unsual. The problem . . . .

I: I'm sorry . . . go any further with the change he was uh you use to make were on the area . . . were responsible for. Am I right?

S: Yea.

I: In the book.

S: Uh Uh

I: Ok. What about the other parts of the book?

S: I have no knowledge of the other parts of the book because

I: But had they been changed by other persons responsible for certain areas?

S: They

I: Have you talked to these—to other people

S: No.

I: responsible for other parts of the book.

S: NO. Because uh I was—I had my hands full with what was going on in my office. That what went on in other offices, I was not checking out.

H: . . . the final book with the provinces the night before.

S: Yea

H: Did any—are there any other areas of the book—did any information come in to you uh of areas that had to be changed.

S: No.

H: Because this was the one book going to the provinces I take it, in the morning.

S: That's right. It was only dealing with my area—with the five areas that Germain Denis was responsible for. Alan Nymark was the one that was dealing with the other areas and putting together. There seems to have been from my observations Alan Nymark was doing something with the provinces and they did up briefing books.

I: Ok.

S: Germain Denis was doing something else.

H: Ok. I want to ask you one other question along that line. If the briefing books were twenty areas and you're boss had five of those areas.

S: Yea. What happened to the other fifteen.

H: No. No. But were all those fifteen in the briefing book that went to the provinces-were the whole twenty areas?

S: No. In my briefing book it was my five areas. When I released them it was my five areas.

I: Ok.

S: Yea.

H: Ok.

I: They did not contain anything else?

S: No.

LAPSE OF SECONDS

S: Ok. Uh. The chain of command in government that has always been there and will always be there is that the Prime Minister's office uh for anything they—The Prime Minister connects to the Minister, the Minister gets his information from the Deputy Minister, the Deputy Minister from the ADM (Assistant Deputy Minister). There has never been a direct, a direct conversation for information from Prime Minister to Assistant Deputy Minister level. It does not work that way—it never has. In the case of Germain Denis there was continuous, continuous, several times a week. I was never allowed to take a lunch break because the Prime Minister would contact Germain Denis directly. Germain Denis.

I: It's not a crime though.

S: No. No. It's not a crime.

I: (Laughs)

S: It was very unusual because why would the Prime Minister contact the ADM (Assistant Deputy Minister) when the Prime Minister had hired Simon Reisman to do the job for him.

I: Uh Uh

S: So why was that not going like this. It was going directly

H: . . . you mean normally the Prime Minister would get a hold of Simon Reisman.

S: Yea. You'd better believe it.

H: Simon Reisman would get hold of Germain Denis and give him instructions.

S: Yes. Exactly.

H: And what you're saying

S: What I'm saying is that the contact was direct between Prime Minister and Germain Denis.

H: How was that made?

S: Through his—it was always a different aide. Mulroney had several aides. I don't remember their names right now, but Germain Denis (Prime Minister) had several aides—and it was always one of the aides that could say the Prime Minister would like to speak to Mr. Denis. Can you arrange it.

H: They would call you.

S: They would call me direct. Yes. They would call me direct and I was the only person in TNO that never could take a lunch break during 1987. As a matter of fact, a lot of people uh

I: Did you witness any conversation between the Prime Minister and

H: . . . .

S: No. The. When I was forced not to take lunch hours in case the Prime Minister called, because the Prime Minister only called during the lunch break. He never called during office hours. It was always during the lunch break and the minute he would call, I had been given advance notice that every time it was the Prime Minister's office that I had to shut Germain Denis' door. That was the only time that Germain Denis ever shut his door when there was a conversation going between him and the Prime Minister. That was the only time that, that door was ever shut. And, plus you can add the fact to that, that I had become quite closely linked to Gordon Ritchie's office who was a Senior Deputy Minister level. I was close to his Executive Assistant and I was also very much appreciated by Gordon Ritchie.

H: Who was the Executive Assistant?

S: Joanne Aube. Now, I. It was normal in government that if you're working for an Assistant Deputy Minister that you have outstanding relations with your Deputy Minister's office and keep them informed of everything at all times. It's the way it has to be for things to work—for the machinery to work. And, I've been in government since 1961 and my ADMs always—we had very close ties with our DM. Just like the DM would have with the Minister. Now when Germain Denis found out that I was having these fabulous relations with the Executive Assistant and Gordon Ritchie I was told to can it and immediately or else. "You are not to have—I don't want that office to know what's happening in this office" and that's a quote, a direct quote that I'll never forget.

H:?   . . . .

S: Because Mrs. Aube can be questioned. Joanne Aube can be questioned. That all she remembers is that all of a sudden—one day I'm her best friend, I'm giving her a present and the next day I had to—I took it—I did something nasty to their offices to break off the ties under orders of Germain Denis because he said 'I don't care how you do it Shelley Ann but that relationship has gotta stop and now.

And I am to break off my relations with Gordon Ritchie's office. I wrote up some nasty note and uh she (Joanne Aube) flared up and ran in to Gordon Ritchie. Gordon Ritchie was all upset. I should have kept a copy of that though. It might still be amongst my stuff because it's what caused the split between the offices, was the note that I wrote to Joanne Aube.

H: What was Gordon Ritchie's role?

S: Gordon Ritchie was uh in the end what I remember—Gordon Ritchie was like a figure head I guess. You know, he—if Simon Reisman couldn't go somewhere Gordon Ritchie went. It was that sort of thing. Of course, they were the ones that were in with Peter Murphy and the other counterpart. While the other people were in what they called working groups you know. But then there would be meetings on a one on one between Simon Ritchie (Reisman) and Peter Murphy.

I: Are there any other people uh are there . . . you and Mr. Von Finckenstein—would know about changes made?

S: Not to my knowledge, because uh Germain Denis was continuously reminding me that no one was to know what was going on in his office and if I ever opened my mouth that I would be finished here in Ottawa.

I: Ok. The only other . . .

H: The only other people that would know are all of the provincial premiers' officers that attended on those briefings and they would all know about the briefing books and they would also, I would expect, have a right to see those briefing books because they're national documents—they're not available but they did have them. So all of those people would be good witnesses to say that those briefing books are not available now.

S: You see those briefing books were part of the negotiating material that were ordered, because it said that the documents—the memo clearly said: 'all documentation used during the Canada-U.S.A. main negotiations were to be returned for—to be catalogued for the Archives. Now you have a year's work of provincial books that

I: What happened . . . put the . . . in the car

S: Yes.

I: What happened.

S: And, I have a witness who was saying that he doesn't remember. On my first trip, Philippe Tessier was the chauffeur to Simon Reisman and a young man that was is known as a real ladies' gentleman you know. He likes women and he's polite too. He can't stand to see a woman carry anything. He wants to open doors. That's the character. Now, I'm coming to the elevator with this heavy Xerox box

I: That was on the first trip . . .

S: and I—he immediately came towards me and offered to carry the box and he also asked me what the hell I was carrying that it was so heavy. I lied and told him it was Random House dictionaries. And, he said you're going to your car with those and I said yes and I said I'm fine and he said 'No No Shelley Ann you cannot carry those boxes you know, I've got carry them. The whole time I knew I didn't have my car keys in my pocket. I only had Germain Denis' car keys because that's where I was going. But this guy is insisting to carry the damn box to my car and I couldn't say well no I'm going to Germain Denis' car because here I have Germain Denis telling me, you know, not to be caught and yet I didn't want to be caught having a witness seeing me put those boxes in my car. I said God if anything ever happened that this stuff got out—I'll be questioned did you ever put the material in your car? I said (to myself) I don't want any witness seeing me putting the stuff in my car so I went down to my car with Phil and I said Oh God! I forgot my car keys, you know, stupid me, I was so preoccupied I forgot my car keys, which was not true—it's just that I couldn't bring him to Germain Denis' car. So I made him—he insisted on waiting and I said No No No go back Simon might need you and he put—I made him put that box under the front of my car and I pretended to go back up to my office. Phil followed me, I couldn't believe it, it was like a nightmare. The guy wouldn't let go. Phil followed me. I rummaged around my purse and finally when he saw me rummaging around my purse he left, but I didn't take my car keys down. I just went back and proceeded with the deed. Now it took me until 6:30 at night to do this.

I: How many boxes.

S: Seven. There were seven boxes and it took me until 6:30 at night to do it in such a way where I wouldn't be suspected. Because during those seven trips you can imagine the number of people—there was a 110 approximately at TNO working on the 17th floor. Imagine the number of people I had to come across who asked me: Shelley Ann—are your leaving. They thought I was moving out.

H: Maybe this gentleman would like to know the names of some of the people that had access to the safe where these books were kept.

S: Germain Denis and I were the only ones with access.

H: Were there any other people that would know what was in that safe?

S: No. Unless Security behind our backs went to check, which would be Guy Marcoux.

H: Guy Marcoux had access to that safe?

S: Guy Marcoux would have had a list of the combinations of each safe. That's a security measure, you know. Guy Marcoux had to have that kind of thing.

H: Guy Marcoux would have known if all those documents were missing?

S: Guy Marcoux would not have known, no.

H: If he had checked the safe he would have known?

S: If he had checked the safe he would have seen negotiating material which was unidentified, the provincial ones. Germain Denis was keeping them in a blank file folder. So, because I guess he must have figured well, if anybody checked

H: How did he . . . in that safe. Each one of them was in a blank file folder.

S: . . . yes, that's right.

H: So that the seven boxes

S: Under agriculture, under the different topics. All agriculture material was together, all subsidies material was together, all

H: The place was large enough so that it could be accessed quite easily by

S: Oh yes it was behind his door. That's where he wanted it because it—it didn't fit well and I wondered at the time because, I'm the one that organized his new office and I had it—I had it facing the door and he said NO. I want it behind the door. "I don't want people watching me when I'm putting stuff in here". I kept saying GEES, there's private and private because at first I didn't know what was going on. There's all these statements, you know, that I keep remembering that—he told well I don't want—I don't want to be seen when I'm putting stuff in and I just thought at the time, well, what a private person, you know. He's one of those. Some people have—unusual quirks I call them. They have these quirks that they're so private they can't bear to be watched doing anything. So, I had put it down to that until I started doctoring the provincial documents. And, when—when I submitted this information to the Public Service Alliance of Canada. You can see by their covering letter what they said.

H: Did you . . . did you submit the information that you told this gentleman today to someone at the—at your union.

S: Yes. Everything was

H: Did they know everything that you told here about those books?

S: Yes. It's all documented.

H: Who did you advise of that and when did you advise of that?

S: When I filed my grievance. I would have to go in to my grievance paper uh. We'd have an approximate date by looking at that covering letter when they returned the documentation to me. But, I had a meeting in there uh about that particular relevant section of AI-5. Uhm there was a Dennis, Dennis. I forget Dennis' last name but there was a Dennis who is still there, Lloyd Fucile and Mary Ramsay.

H: Lloyd Fucile, F U S S

S: F U, no F U C I L E

H: F U C I L E, Dennis and what's the other person's name.

S: Mary Ramsay was there.

H: And were these people told about the briefing book changes and all this stuff that you were doing?

S: Yes they were told verbally like you were told. There is one portion that I told you verbally and there's one portion that I told them verbally because I was scared to death to put it on paper.

H: When did this take place? When you told these people.

S: Ok. When I filed, when I filed the grievance uh and he would have to look at that covering letter because it would be several weeks before that letter returning my document.

H: What date was that?

S: I don't remember because I haven't looked at the letter. It's in your office.

H: Ok. Well I can provide the letter.

I: . . . .

S: Wasn't that part of the package though that went out with that letter. Return of the document. The letter that you sent to Inkster and to the premiers.

H: To . . .

S: This was the letter on the top from the PSAC.

H: Ok. So you have the date then.

I: . . . .

S: He wouldn't. I wanted to hire someone to help me but he wouldn't let me.

I: Who wrote the briefing books?

S: Who wrote the briefing books? He

I: . . . .

S: No. For each topic he had a man that would be a head of section ok that would—the head of section, you see, like the head of section for Tariffs was a Kevin Gore. The head of section for Agriculture was Mike Gifford. The head of section for subsidies was Germain Denis himself. Intellectual Property was a John Curtis.

I: Can you repeat that to me? Agriculture

S: Mike Gifford

I: Mike Gifford

S: Yea

I: Is he still at

S: He's still with Germain Denis. The whole bunch of them—he gave them permanent jobs for life with the Multilateral Trade.

I: Tariffs?

S: Tariffs, Kevin Gore.

H: . . . .

I: Ok. Intellectual Property?

S: John Curtis.

H: You have five areas that you . . . before?

S: Ok. I'll go over—we've got Agriculture, Tariffs, Ok, Government Procurement.

I: Subsidies, Agriculture

S: No No you don't have Government Procurement.

I: Ok.

S: Bob Martin

H: They drafted all the material for those books?

S: They would—they would. Now this is where it gets interesting. They would—they were told that they could never do a final version which got—which caused internal fighting. He (Denis) would get them to do up a draft but he insisted that only he could make the changes to their draft which caused me all the (Tape goes blank for a few seconds)

N.B.   Since this transcript has been made from a copy and not the original tape it seems that at this point the person copying the tape did not pay close attention and repeated the following from * to *.

*

S: Tariffs. Ok Government Procurement.

I: Tariffs, Agriculture

S: No—No you don't have Government Procurement

I: Ok

S: Bob Martin

H: They drafted all of the material for those books.

S: They would—they would. Now this is where it gets interesting. They would—they were told that they could never do a final version which got—which caused internal fighting uh. He (Denis) would get them to do up a draft, but he insisted that only he could make the changes to their draft, which caused me all the * additional work because I wanted to give—after they provided Germain with the draft ok

H: — · — · — · — · — · — · — · — · —

S: Yea

H: These people would be asked to make a draft of a section of the . . . .

S: Yes.

H: Now the briefing book. That would then—what would happen to the document after they had completed their first draft?

S: Once they completed that draft the draft was brought to me to give to Germain Denis. Germain Denis would make all kinds of adjustments to their draft. This is normal. Ok. But then what was not the normal which happened with all the other sections is that that the normal would be that I would then take those changes of each area; give them back to the guy who drafted it and his secretary should have been making the changes because she's the one that would have the whole thing in her computer. You know the secretary would input this draft in her computer. I wouldn't have it in my computer so

I: Are you saying that this was kept from the others, the assistants

S: Well, that's exactly what would happen. Is that he made me and the secretaries were all insulted—"I should be doing this". It was causing me ten hours of extra work all the time, you know. I was in there til all hours because of this—because he would not let his people or their secretaries see the changes that he was making. The changes were completely controlled by him (Denis) with me being the only one that I would—I had an access—I didn't have to get their diskettes. They were—I had access by coding in certain numbers to link. Let's say for Bob Martin's area we were working on. I would link up—without their knowledge I would be able to link up to her computer, copy the material onto mine and make the changes that Germain had done. And that's how it went throughout the whole thing. And these—Bob Martin, in the end, almost had a nervous breakdown because he knew what was going on and he left.

I: Yea

S: . . . . I kid you not. The man got very ill. I know why a lot of people got very ill there. I mean, I lived through it.

I: So he's no longer with Denis.

S: No, he's the only one. The others all

I: Do you have an address for him or phone number or

S: I have nothing on that man. But he must be . . . it was Robert J. Martin so he must be in the phone book, he must be, you know. I don't know where he is because I've been out of the country so where he landed after I left that place. I don't know. I wasn't keeping track.

I: Do you recall. Let's say ah Mr. ah Mr. Denis was responsible for the changes on drafts and he was responsible to the extent to not—or keep it for himself, with your assistance.

S: Uh Uh

I: That could be the instructions he received.

H: Who were the bosses then?

S: Ok

H: The chain of command.

S: Yes

H: Who was the chain of command for these various five heads for these departments?

S: Ok

H: Who would be their boss?

S: Germain Denis.

H: Germain Denis was their boss.

S: Their boss.

H: Was anybody else their boss?

S: NO. Just Germain Denis.

I: So, let's say Denis received instructions from higher not to tell any of the assistants about the changes he was making on the drafts.

S: Well, I'm sure that he did receive such instructions.

I: It doesn't mean its criminal. There could be a reason for that. That's what I want to hear from you. Is there any reason for that?

S: Well I—it wasn't that, that bothered me it was the fact of the operation.

I: . . . there's no reason for that—for the change.

H: She told you. She just said to you, the normal procedure would be—they would make the changes under their heading, ok. Then they would come to, in the normal procedure come to her, she would give them to Mr. Germain Denis

S: And they (the drafts) should have been returned there

H: The normal procedure would have been—return them to their head of the department to make the changes on their computer and then they would go in to the system.

S: I had to do the job of five secretaries.

I: Well it could be so highly secret that uh somebody in the chain of command wanted to

S: It shouldn't have been because these were the people that were negotiating in the working groups A. B. Germain

H: These were the people that were negotiating with the Americans in the Working Groups.

S: Yes. These people went to the Working Groups ok, but what went in to the book was after the Working Group. The Working Group would take place. They would draft up what had happened in the Working Group, ok. They would come back from the Working Group. They would draft up for Germain Denis what had happened. And, that—from that point Germain Denis . . . everything in and nobody could touch it again. And what was abnormal and I tell you this very seriously was that he was not reporting to Gordon Ritchie the way he was supposed to. He was only the ADM, Gordon Ritchie was his boss and he (Denis) didn't want his boss to know anything of what was going on in that office. Now you explain that to me. If you think that I have no reason to suspect that something was wrong. I would have to be awfully stupid.

I: I'm sure it happened and—in all departments that sometimes a boss will skip two or three bosses in the chain of command and will get to the employee he wants to talk to and say I want this done this and this and this and then you report to me, not to your boss.

S: What really—what

I: You've got to know that.

S: . . . .

I: . . . the department

S: I have worked for ADMs and Deputy Ministers level all my life.

I: Yes

S: And A, one—maybe in a three year period there would be an instance where the DM felt that he would have to go directly to a person to handle something. But, here we are talking about negotiations where everybody was a team and all information had to be communicated. And, information was not communicated. We are talking not a government office where—where communication isn't absolutely essential—sure a Deputy Minister will sometimes go to uh—that somebody has reported to a Deputy Minister that so and so has done something wrong—they're doing something that's not right. The Deputy Minister sometimes will skip that chain of command—have the guy brought in and question him directly because some guys—some deputy ministers are not egotistical and therefore will break the chain of command and they will deal with that person. I know because I worked with such a thing when there was a guy that was at External Affairs that was accused of uh defrauding government of overtime money. He was claiming for time that he wasn't doing. The guy went—instead of going through

I: I'm sure . . .

H: Ok I'm going to ask a question.

S: The Free Trade Negotiations was team work.

H: I wanna ask a question. You said you worked for many ADMs throughout the years. How many years?

S: '61 to '92.

H: Ok. Now, were there any times during that period of time where there was direct communication by the ADM on a regular basis with the Prime Minister.

S: Never

H: Never

S: Never, never, never. NO. I'll swear to that. I will swear to that. They never made me uh . . . these guys never had direct contact with the Prime Minister. Because, I know, because of the material they were submitting to their Deputy Ministers, which went from their Deputy Ministers on to the Minister.

H: So, this was highly unusual that a

S: Why do you think I was there

H: . . . with the Prime Minister

S: Uh

I: It might be unusual but it doesn't mean there's something wrong or something

H: . . . where they should be . . . (laughter)

S: There's something very wrong here.

I: I don't think . . . unusual . . . the Deputy

S: No. What I have is not the fact that the phone calls but the fact that the books were altered and that nobody will ever make me say otherwise when I know what I saw and I know the hell that I went through.

I: . . . happened

S: It happened.

I: It happened.

S: . . . if it was not illegal why was I under continued threats?

I: From?

S: From Germain Denis. Yes. If it was legal what he was doing, you know, if everything was on the up and up—if he was doing nothing wrong, like your suggesting, and then why did he have to threaten me?

I: You claim to various threats.

S: Ok. Every time that I had to do something illicit I was reminded that I could be—that me and my family could be totally destroyed; B, on other occasions it would not be such a severe threat it would be "well you realize what I can do to you—I would ensure that you never work for Government or get a job in this city again, as long as you live".

I: Ok

S: And you'd better keep your mouth shut. And, Germain Denis was the type that spoke rudely. He was not refined. I'm using his language right now when I'm speaking to you. This is not my language.

H: Any other threats?

S: No. It was always the job and it was always that he could destroy my family and I.

H: Ok. Now did he in fact as a result of those threats—he completed those threats because you came back last December (1992) and you've never had a job (since).

S: That's right.

H: Can you tell me who the Ambassador of Switzerland was at that particular time? And who that friend was?

S:	Yes. Germain Denis' best friend and the Deputy Minister he was reporting to at External Affairs during this period of 1987 was Gerald E. Shannon. Now I went to—Gerald E. Shannon was suddenly appointed, even though he was not a foreign service diplomat, he was appointed as Ambassador to the Permanent Mission of Canada to the United Nations in Geneva, Switzerland. I was posted to Geneva, Switzerland and I—and I was brought back after fifteen months, even though I was suppose to be there four years because of an ongoing salem type witch hunt against me and my children. Everything got documented on a monthly basis—everything was sent to the Public Service Alliance, Mr. Lloyd Fucile on what they were doing to me. And, Mr. Fucile kept saying "as long as they're doing it verbally we can do nothing and I was put through—ostracized—everyone at that Mission was told not to come near me—that I was a very dangerous person to be near. So, I spent fifteen months in Switzerland having no friends, being totally ostracized by everyone in that Mission. By a—by the Deputy Permanent Representative—I had been there two weeks when I was told {I'm a senior secretary which is a SCY-4 level and I've been with External Affairs for 30 years} and I was told that I would not even qualify as a SCY-1, I was totally incompetent and that I should be returned to Canada immediately because I didn't even have any knowledge of French, I couldn't handle senior officials. I mean I was put down to the ground two weeks after my arrival.

I:	From them.

H:	. . . just for a second. Came back in December and you were getting $4,000.00 a month at that time?

S:	Yes. I was—with all the foreign service benefits it made my salary approximately $4,000.00 a month compared to the $1800 that I earn here, in Ottawa.

H: Ok. And then when you came back to Ottawa. What happened then to complete the threat of you not having a job or being able to work with government. When was the next completion of that threat?

S: It was

H: How much money did you get when you came back in December?

S: When I came back in December there was a hearing that was held and I was told, for operational reasons

H: What was that?

S: . . . .

H: I don't know . . . wasted a lot of time.

S: A December 10 (1992) hearing on December 10. At the December 10 hearing they did not go over my documentation on the reports of the harassment. They asked me three questions: I was asked 1) When did you join this Department? and I said August 1961.

TAPE 2: CONCLUSION

S: This one is the conclusion

I: Where was this taking place?

S: . . . Ottawa and then Mr. John McCann of Staff Relations said 'Well we'll have to bring you back to Ottawa, but I think the best thing under her circumstances uh to keep her out of the limelight in this department (Department of External Affairs) for awhile it would be better to send her off on secondment. So I agreed, to that. I said Ok, I think it's a good idea for a year or two for me to be off on secondment to, you know, to stop the gossip in the department.

H: They kept your salary down to how much?

S: My salary in December was cut down to $1800.00 from $4,000.00.

H: Ok

S: Then it was—later on it was cut down

H: When was later on? Tell me what later on meant.

S: Later on meant, in April

H: Of this year (1993)

S: Of this year

H: After you'd come to see me.

S: Yes—No, after I came to see you or was it before? March or April suddenly I saw that in my bank account because I am on one of those automatic deposits. Uh I had a posting loan which I received to go overseas, which I had the four years with the $4,000.00 to pay off. When I came—whey they brought me back to Ottawa—NOT AT MY REQUEST, but they brought me back. They started the deductions on—they had given me—they were supposed to give me until May 31st to make arrangements to pay back the posting loan at minimal cost to me, because obviously I couldn't pay it back at $600.00 a month that I was paying then when I was receiving $4,000.00. With $1800.00 I was affording maybe $50/$100.00 a month, but they gave me four months to arrange this. Well, two months before the four months were up, which the four months were up on May 31st. Sometime in March I arrived at the bank and my salary had been cut from every second week from $995.00 down to $627.00

H: It had come down by $600.00.

S: It had come down by about $600.00 a month again.

H: And you didn't work from December (1992) on.

S: I haven't work from December 7 to present day (presently means of of today's date, September 13, 1993) and they are telling me that I am not hireable—nobody wants to employ me.

H: OK. Is that exactly what Germain Denis said to you about the employment.

S: No. No. Germain Denis has had nothing to do

H: But when he threatened you.

S: Oh when he threatened me

H: He did say

S: Yes he did.

H: What did he say?

S: 'That I would never be able to be employed in Ottawa again or in government'.

H: Isn't this what they are saying to you today.

S: And now, the Personnel Office (of External Affairs) is telling me that nobody will hire me—they can't find me a job quote unquote.

H: I think you have enough evidence.

I: Just go ahead.

S: And I am being paid my salary to sit home and watch TV since December 7 (1992).

H: Unemployable.

S: Unemployable.

I: So, you receive a $1200.00 a month.

H: Right now.

S: Right up to

I: From $4,000.0 to $1800

S: Yes then

I: Down to $1200.00

H: And then she goes out the door

S: And then the next step would be out the door.

H: I must say that since

S: your letter

H: that since my letter to the various premiers questioning the verocity of the Government of Canada, I have been in contact with the Head Counsel for External Affairs and they have advised me, I don't know whether they are going to do anything, but I have told them, because there was Minutes of Settlement at the time because of a sexual harassment against my client by Mr. Germain Denis and you must know that Mr. Germain Denis' best friend was the Ambassador in Switzerland and he was going to get this lady whether—someway or other because of that fact—of the sexual harassment by Germain Denis. He finally did and she's back in Canada and uh I think there's enough evidence now that in fact—that the people at External Affairs I have asked them for re-instatement of the Minutes of Settlement at $4,000.00 a month and I suspect that there's meetings going on about that regularly and because it is in fact—a threat is being carried by Germain Denis from whoever he is taking his authority from, which I would suggest to you is the Prime Minister of Canada. She was going to be out of the country and if she didn't keep her mouth shut she would be . . . and that's exactly where she is. Now. General Counsel of External Affairs, because when I sent a letter with regard to the Minutes of Settlement that the Federal Government and had breached, I sent a copy to Barbara McDougall (Minister of External Affairs), as well as to the various other people involved in this matter and asked 'is this the way you treat employees in the Government of Canada? Ok, and since then I have had one conversation with him (Richard Fuitowski, Legal Counsel for External Affairs) and I haven't received his reply yet because I have a course of action for my client because they have not lived up to their Minutes of Settlement. Since—from Mr. Germain Denis, sexually harassed her, etc. and I don't know why he did that, but it's that type of a person we're dealing with here and that in fact also said to her when he was doing a lot of other illegal things such as sexual harassment, that she was to be—that she had better do as she's told or she would be fired and therefore she did everything he wanted and that included making up all the changes on all of these agreements (free trade) etc. that were made. He was doing something illegal again, and used the same methods and at the end she's out of a job.

I: That would include . . . .

H: Now whether he was in this on his own or whether this was the Prime Minister advising Mr. Gemain Denis what the hell to do, then I would suggest to you that it was the Prime Minister that was advising Germain Denis of all the changes that were going on in the Free Trade Agreement and what was having to be placed before the provincial people because he wanted a hands-on approach to his Prime Ministership which he got and then he (Denis) would tell her what to put in. He (the Prime Minister) would tell Germain Denis what to put in these documents for the premiers to make them happy because that's what had to be done to get the Free Trade Agreement through.

I: I don't see anything wrong.

H: But, they have a, but they have with this person (Shelley Ann Clark) completed their threat.

S: The Minutes of Settlement were signed. What is interesting is that the Minutes of Settlement were signed by a senior lawyer of Treasury Board (Harvey Newman). Not just with External Affairs. They could not prove, according to their report my witnesses that I told that I was being sexually harassed by Germain Denis and the proposal that he made to me. He wanted to set me up in a house behind External Affairs across the river in New Edinburgh and there's a row of white houses there. He wanted to set me up in one of those white houses because he wanted to be able to run over at lunch time ok. Now, the witnesses that I had reported this to. When they were questioned said 'Oh we don't remember—We don't remember'. So

H: What witnesses?

S: Oh, there was Joanne Aube the EA to Gordon Ritchie, there was a clerk, (Lorraine Bachs—still employed by Germain Denis). What was her name—I have—when I sit down on my own quietly I will remember the name. But right now, uh I—Nathalie Grenier was a main witness and Lorraine Bachs because I told both of those ladies what he was threatening me with. I told them—I said he's threatened that if I don't agree to this I'm gonna—you know, he's going to . . . he's gonna have me out of government. And, those two ladies, in particular I told Nathalie Grenier and Lorraine Bachs. Lorraine Bachs

H: Those were the threats that he used because he was trying to compromise her because of the uh

S: If I would have agreed to go to bed with him I was compromised.

H: She was not only compromised but he was trying to compromise her because she was making changes in the Free Trade Agreement and making changes there were illegal ok. So it suited him very nicely.

I: And you never heard what happened to the books after these trips to the trunk of his car?

S: I was uh

H/I: (laughter)

S: (laughter)

H: I would suggest for————————to look in . . . .

S: . . . .

H: No. No.

S/H/I: . . . (more laughter)

H: You may find those in the Prime Minister's residence because very often people like to keep things . . . communication with these two people.

S: I mean, I'm the one—I should add this—is that I'm the one which is against, which is unbelievable—on the morning. On the Sunday night, at midnight, on October 2nd (1987) they (Reisman and his team) came back from Washington

H: What year?

S: 1987. October 2nd, (3rd) 1987 they came back at midnight at night and I was called at home and I was told to be there very early the next morning because we had to prepare for the press conference that Simon was going to give. So, I went in there the next morning and sent them off and I knew that Germain Denis had shown me the summarized version that the Prime Minister was going to table. This was the Monday and the Prime Minister had said that he was going to table it on the Friday. So, Germain Denis takes off with the original, I know it was the original because all the signatures on each page were in different colours. He showed me the original and he said I've got it in my brief case and I'm going to the Conference Centre with it. He took off for the Conference Centre. He hadn't been there for 10 minutes and the Prime Minister's aide called me and said "the Prime Minister wants to talk to Germain Denis" and I said "I'm sorry, he's already gone to the Conference Centre". He said: 'Well, Shelley Ann you have to do us a favour, the Prime Minister has decided that he wants that Agreement here within twenty minutes because he's going to table it in the house this morning (this was October 4, 1987). I said 'fine I know where it is—I'll get it and I took a taxi cab—made the guy go through red lights and everything because I said the Prime Minister is wanting this and the minute I used the words Prime Minister, the guy just broke all traffic regulations—got me there. We—so the reporters would not see us we sat down on the ground and I opened my brief case and he opened his (Denis) and he slipped the Agreement into my brief case. I went straight to the Prime Minister's office and obviously the Security had been advised downstairs because I didn't have to present credentials or anything—they said "Shelley Ann Clark" and I said "Yes" and they said "Come" (laughter). Then I was swished upstairs and to my shock, Mulroney was standing there with two of his aides leaning against the column in front of his office, waiting for this.

H: Why had Germain Denis taken this to the Conference Centre?

S: I don't know. Because he couldn't release it until the Prime Minister tabled it.

H: It was a signed document and it was out of the office in his hands (Denis') at the Conference Centre.

S: That's right.

H: Under security.

S: Yes.

I: And, where was his office at that time?

S: 17th floor, TNO. We were still there. This is '87 now, we didn't move out until the fall of '88. They didn't move out til the fall of '88. Now

I: 50 O'Connor

S: 50 O'Connor, 17th floor.

H: There was a lot of security. So what was going on at the Conference Centre that he (Denis) took it over

S: Well, there was about 200 journalists there, TV cameras and everything for Simon Reisman's announcement that all was signed.

I: Were all people that were responsible for the negotiations, areas of the negotiations in the same building?

S: Yes.

I: 50 O'Conner.

S: They were all on the 17th floor. Not the 18—not the 19th. They—we had the entire building from one street to the other, that whole floor. The building started at O'Connor and it finished up . . . .

I: . . . Germain Denis was reporting to Gordon Ritchie.

S: Yes. He was the only one

I: But, according to you he was not reporting too much to Mr. Ritchie.

S: He would go to—Once

I: . . . the next boss who was?

S: Well, he was reporting directly to the Prime Minister. Because at the—once a week Gordon Ritchie would have what he called his Round Table. He was known for that. He was a Deputy Minister in Government before and he was known for his Round Table meetings. And, at these Round Table meetings which took place once a week, because all his Assistant Chief Negotiators had to go in there and report. Now, Germain Denis made it sometimes, didn't make it other times, which would annoy Ritchie and when he did make it—the EA who was, when she was my friend, before he made me break up the friendship saw him at those meetings and she would come back to me and report that "How come your boss has nothing to say?". Isn't he doing any work over there?" Apparently, according to her Germain would play—he had his shoe on and off and everybody else, you know, was reporting very professionally and all that. Germain would say—this is from the EA that sat in on all the meetings (Ritchie's meetings). She was there. She watched it and I said "he was playing with his shoes"—she said "Oh yes, he puts them on and off" and she said—he said so little that we're wondering if he's doing any work, what is he doing in that office of yours, she said. Because she knew I was putting in all these hours and they were asking me why are you not submitting overtime? Are you crazy? You'd be making a bundle. And, I said, Germain does not want to approve my overtime. You tell me—and that's another thing that you should really note is that I was told that "I don't want anybody knowing that you're putting in these hours and at what time.—So you are not to claim any overtime".

H: Except, for in the Minute Book (Appointment Book) in the Minutes

S: I had started. The appointment book I was keeping for him I had started writing in red the time I would arrive in the morning and the time I left at night. And, the minute he saw that, you're going to see that from that point on it is blank because he forbidded me to note it.

I: Uh uh

S: You can see, that earlier on when I was with Multilateral Trade, when I was doing Multilateral Trade with him, my overtime is all noted.

H: Ok. Just a minute. You were doing Multilateral Trade with Germain Denis.

S: Yes. From July of '86 right through to December

H: Ok. You're sure this gentleman (Inspector Droz) can find out that you were paid overtime during that period.

S: Oh yes because External Affairs has overtime records.

H: OK

S: And, when I did overtime during that period I was paid for it. The only overtime that I was paid for uh during the Free Trade was the one time when everybody was brought in for the entire weekend. There was a big rush at the end and everyone was brought in for that weekend. We were told—I was told that (by Denis) "that yes you better do like the others for this time" because the order had come from Reisman and Ritchie that everybody was to claim that weekend as overtime and I had to do like the rest because it would have looked very strange if I hadn't. So that one time he allowed me. There was one or two occasions where he allowed me to do it (near the end) because everybody else did it and that can be verified in the books. All people working there during that time claimed overtime, but where is Shelley Ann Clark's overtime? The people that were doing a lot—there was a typing pool, ok where Word Processor Operators were doing the bulk of the final, the legal . . . . Boy! they made a fortune in overtime. They were buying themselves new TVS and fridges and they were entitled to it. They were putting in their hours. I'm putting in those hours of 18 hour days. It broke up my marriage—my husband that I couldn't tell him why I was going there at that hour of the night though I was having an affair. Cause imagine your wife leaving and not giving you a reason and leaving at 11 o'clock at night and becoming back at four and five in the morning and being tight lipped—very closed up—wouldn't say anything and I wasn't having an affair—I couldn't invent a lover because he might have hired a detective and found out there was no lover. I could not afford to be followed by a jealous husband—by a jealous husband hiring a detective to see where I was going at 11 o'clock at night. So I kept my shut. And my ex-husband is prepared to testify in Court all those times that I left the house—a phone call would come—I would leave the house around 11 p.m. and not show up until four and five in the morning and then I had to appear in the office for eight or eight-thirty the next morning and pretend that I wasn't tired and that everything was fine. I was not allowed to say what I had done. Secretaries that were working around me—they'd say, 'Shelley Ann you look awful, what the hell are you doing—they were making jokes "Are you having an affair on your husband and you're staying up all night—what the heck are you up to? You know. I don't know how many people said that to me because I was going in—you can imagine, after awhile of doing that business of being there until four and five and at 8 o'clock I'm back. These other people didn't know that I had worked all night. I looked like hell. As, a matter of fact, there is even further evidence of what I'm telling you. I came down at one point from exhaustion, I came down with pneumonia from exhaustion and I was off for several weeks then.

H: Who is your witness?

S: I have the doctor. It was a Dr. Chamya that had to look after me and I went down. I went down and Denis was not there and it was Gordon Ritchie and his EA that came to my rescue because I almost passed out at their doorstep. And they said—they couldn't figure out what I was doing because they saw me leave at the same time as the rest of them around six/six-thirty. Joanne Aube and I, while we had allowed the friendship to go on, she and I would leave at the same time. Six-Six-thirty was our normal time. What they didn't know was that I was coming back in later on.

I: Ok. Can I get a copy of this tape?

H: Wait until we get it made. I'll go with you.

*   *   *

Signature witnessed by: Signed by:
Margaret Bowly, CABL   Shelley Ann Clark

Chapter 27

What Happens to Whistleblowers
when there is No Act to protect them

All of my efforts to let Canadians know what had happened to "OUR" country and all the pressure that I applied to get the people who had the power to make a difference by investigating the sale of "OUR" country became a dead end for all Canadians, but not for me.

As a result, I have been hounded for years with death threats, telephones being tapped, hacking of my website, residences broken into and ransacked, checked luggage on airplanes always searched and their arrival delayed, harassment at work and all income completely cut off by both my employer, the Department of Foreign Affairs and International Trade Canada and my health insurance company.

Why? All because of the existence of the "Implementation Scheme". "They" insisted on believing that I had stolen a copy because "they" felt I had every opportunity to do so. "They" as usual underestimated me. I would never be stupid enough to steal a copy of such a document. To do so would have been the end of my existence. However, the existence of this document was subsequently confirmed by a Member of the United States Negotiating Team who attended one of my public speaking engagements. This individual was in the audience when I publicly exposed the sale of our country in Edmonton, Alberta in February 1994.

In Volume II—"Fighting Shadows" I will be exposing in detail every ploy that was orchaestrated against me, as well as exposing the present judicial system that we have in this country. We now live in a country where democracy is just an illusion. "OUR" Constitution is in CRISIS.

What are Canadians willing to do to take back "OUR" country? Unfortunately, only 10% care enough to take on the battle and as everyone knows that number is not sufficient. To take on this huge battle we need 80% of Canadians to fight back and TAKE BACK WHAT IS THEIRS. "WE" have already become a country of KINGS AND SERFS.

SYNOPSIS
By
Shelley Ann Clark

- **September 1986 to October 1987**. My ordered falsification of Canada-U.S. Free Trade Briefing Books, used to surreptitiously garner support from the Provincial Premiers.

- **September 1986 to July 1988**. Repeated sexual harassment and commensurate threats to my career by Germain Denis, third in command at the Free Trade Negotiations Office at the Department of Foreign Affairs and International Trade (DFAIT).

- **Fall of 1986**. American owned GEAC Computer system worth $1.2 million removed from the Trade Negotiations Office (TNO) due to the discovery, by me, that GEAC had an American President at the helm. I discovered and blew the whistle internally, that this American President had a "God Password" that could access all materials contained in the 110 TNO computers including Reisman's. All material entered into the system was compromised, e.g. Top Secret Memoranda to Cabinet, all strategies and working papers could be accessed by the Americans. I was lauded by Reisman and Ritchie for my discovery, but strangely Germain Denis was outraged by it. The removal of this system, so early on, cost the taxpayers $1.2 million.

- **March 1988.** Ordered, by Germain Denis, under threat of destroying my career if I did not comply, to covertly remove key Free Trade documents, including the Implementation Scheme for the merger of Canada and the U.S., and to place them in the trunk of his car.

- **July 1988.** Retaliatory foreign diplomatic posting, including my removal from Ottawa to the Permanent Mission of Canada to the United Nations in New York City**, moments** after filing my initially verbal sexual harassment complaint with the departmental personnel officer. After this incident I filed a complaint with my union, PSAC.

- **1989.** DFAIT offers Ambassadorship to Third World Country. It took my union, PSAC, one year to get an agreement from DFAIT to send me to a Western World Country instead. {Refer to attached Minutes of Settlement}.

- **June 1990**. Arrived in Vienna, Austria for a one year assignment.

- **August 1990** Break in and ran sacking of my private residence in Vienna; probably motivated by the government's search/retrieval of the "Implementation Scheme", designed to merge Canada with the United States, which was part of the key documents removed to the trunk of Denis's car.

- Unexplained illness in Vienna (with the above-mentioned ransacking of my residence, investigated by th Austrian State Police) and Ambassador David Peel's refusal to launch the necessary protocol for my access to the

American Embassy's in-house physician, after denying my request to see the local Canadian Immigration doctor.

- **November 1990.** Under instructions from Human Resources at DFAIT headquarters, Ambassador Peel is ordered to return me to Ottawa immediately.

- **January 1991.** Residence in Ottawa is ran sacked.

- **August 1991.** Arrive in Geneva, Switzerland for my second assignment. This assignment was to last from 4 to 5 years.

- **December 1992.** After enduring psychological warfare and emotional abuse for a period of sixteen (16) months by everyone at the Canadian Permanent Mission of Canada to the United Nations, my union demanded my return to Ottawa.

- **December 1992 to October 1993.** DFAIT ordered me to stay at home with full pay. In October 1993, after Jean Chretien won the election for the Liberals and became Prime Minister, he ordered DFAIT_to bring me back to the department in a high profile position as the Administrator for the United Nations World Summit on Social Development.

SAGA continues in Volume II—Fighting Shadows—"You can see them, but you can't touch them" The True Story of a Whistleblower.

CHAPTER 28

CANADIAN CONSTITUTION IN "CRISIS"

"An Open Letter to the Prime Minister of Canada"

Chapter 28

Canadian Constitution in "CRISIS"

"An Open Letter to the Prime Minister of Canada":

Mr. Prime Minister:

"We, the People" of Canada, whose origins began in this country reject "your" vision for OUR country. "We" have assembled across this country to resist your efforts of forever changing OUR constitution and undermining OUR freedom.

It is obvious that you are NOT hearing US, since you have not acknowledged OUR message.

Former U.S. President Wilson once said, a leader's ear must ring with the voices of the people. The time has now come for you to lean over and listen to what the people of this great country of ours needs you to hear.

OUR greatest treasure is OUR "freedom". WE no longer want to have our hands tied. WE want the ability to think and act without the restraints that have been imposed upon us. A natural result of freedom is individual responsibility. WE believe in the power of individuals.

OUR soldiers went to war and many gave their lives so that WE would have a FREE CANADA. It is unfortunate that, that work is not finished, yet you continue to lead US, the people of Canada deeper and deeper into your vortex, where you believe that we will never be able to get out. Mr. Prime Minister, you are wrong. WE shall prevail and we shall win back OUR freedom.

FREEDOM is the capacity for self-determination and WE the People of Canada are determined.

FREEDOM is NOT an entity. It is a condition, and conditions can change. FREEDOM can expand, but it can also shrink.

You promised Canadians change when you took office, Mr. Prime Minister, but turning US into slaves is not the kind of change WE wanted or will accept.

We know that the New World Order has already put into effect, a plan to eliminate the middle class and return US to a world where there exists only Kings and Serfs.

You, Mr. Prime Minister have:

- ✓ Expanded government
- ✓ Violated OUR constitution
- ✓ Confounded laws
- ✓ Seized private industry
- ✓ Destroyed jobs
- ✓ Perverted our economy
- ✓ Curtailed free speech
- ✓ Weakened our national security and
- ✓ Endangered OUR Sovereignty

When you compromised Canada's cultural, legal and economic institutions, you ensured that our children would never have the same quality of life that we enjoyed in the past.

Through generational theft, you are robbing the unborn of opportunities that they are entitled to because they were born Canadians.

THIS IS NOT ACCEPTABLE.

NOT IN CANADA.
We accept the challenge and WE will be assembling across Canada to deliver OUR message as often and in every way we can.

Mr. Prime Minister we have taken a vow that WE, AS A PROUD CANADIAN NATION will resist your coercive style of governing.

PATRIOTS will NOT STAND silent as you attempt to dismantle what WE believe to be the greatest nation on earth.

WE will protect Canada and it's outstanding and rare qualities will prevail.

Sincerely,

"WE" The People of Canada

Biography
of
Shelley Ann Clark

"The Pen is Mightier than the Sword"

Shelley Ann Clark was born in Ottawa's Embassy Row and had the great advantage of socializing at a very early age with Ottawa's elite Anglophone and Francophone communities and was therefore fluent in both official languages of her home country at the very early age of 4 years old.

In 1961, months prior to receiving her degree in business administration, she was recruited by the Department of Foreign Affairs and International Trade (aka External Affairs). Aside from taking "Parenthood Leave", her entire career was associated with this department. Due to Shelley Ann's competence with protocol, public relations, her ease at learning foreign languages and her ease with literary expression, she was frequently on loan to foreign governments.

Shelley Ann in 1991 was presented with an award by the Secretary of State for External Affairs, the Honorable Joe Clark. The award was given to her "In recognition of your contribution to the Department of External Affairs Kuwait Task Force during the Gulf Crisis, 1990-1991".

Shelley Ann's first book was titled "How to Become a Professional Secretary". She also wrote an instruction manual on how to organize and manage an executive's office. These books were written at the request of a local high tech company who needed to train their employees who were on the production line but wished to move up in the ranks and qualify for an office job. Reportedly, these were so popular and effective that the parent company in the United States requested copies for their employees.

Shelley Ann also served as a guest speaker and as a panelist on radio talk show debates. A frequent issue was "Honesty in Government." She has a proven record in this area.

Between 1980 and 1982, she served as an Administrative Assistant to Senator Doris Anderson when Anderson was the President of the Advisory Council on the Status of Women. Senator Anderson also served as Editor of Chatelaine Magazine.

Shelley Ann exposed a "coup" planned by Anderson's Executive, led and supported by Federal Cabinet Minister, Lloyd Axeworthy. Axeworthy and his band of merry widows plotted to de-throne Anderson by attempting to cancel the National Women's Conference that was to meet on Parliament Hill to demand that women from across Canada be involved in the "repatriation" of the Canadian Constitution.

This exposé made Shelley Ann a household name as she was front page news in every newspaper across the country. CBC's "Fifth Estate's" television program did a documentary on her story. The attached ELMSLIE CARTOON "I Believe he's Axe-worthy", depicting the story was presented to Members of Parliament with the Honorable Flora Macdonald hosting. This cartoon was reproduced from the description of the events as seen through Shelley Ann's eyes.

Shelley Ann Clark is an avowed anti-corruption activist. She does not tolerate the theft of public resources by people entrusted with high office. She never sold her silence for a share of the loot. Perhaps the most noteworthy example took place in 1967 when she worked as Executive Assistant to the Commissioner of Expo 67 and Ambassador representing the small African nation of the Belgian Congo. During the performance of her duties she discovered that the previous Ambassador had been systematically looting the fragile economy of this central African nation. Her reaction was not to ask for "hush-money". Instead, she launched an investigation and played a major role in the arrest and subsequent conviction of the ring leader. Shelley Ann Clark will not remain silent in the shadow of corruption.

The current issue, "FREE TRADE", is by far the most significant in her remarkable career. As a Free Trade official during the Canada and the United States Free Trade Negotiations between 1986 and 1988, she became aware of astounding misrepresentations made to the Provincial Premiers, along with the unauthorized shredding and covert disappearance of key documents.

In 1993, Shelley Ann ran in the Canadian Federal Election for a seat in the House of Commons. Shelley Ann used this opportunity to communicate to Canadians all across Canada that their country had been sold under a FREE TRADE CHARADE with the United States.

In 1994, Shelley Ann, at the invitation of Canadians, was a guest speaker across Canada. Since the mainstream media would not report or investigate her allegations, she took this opportunity to bring the information to Canadians.

This cartoon became famous when it appeared on the front page of the mainstream media across the country that led to CBC doing a documentary on "the fifth estate" covering this story. A replica of this cartoon was presented to all MP's in the House of Commons at a tea party hosted by me and the Honourable Flora McDonald.

"I BELIEVE HE'S AXE-WORTHY"

APPENDIX "A"

Memo assigning proof readers
for the final text of the
Canada-U.S. Free Trade Agreement

Government   Gouvernement
of Canada   du Canada

M E M O R A N D U M
N O T E D E S E R V I C E

DATE: 9 Dec. 1987

TO/DEST: Distribution

FROM/DE: Meriel V.M. Bradford

SUBJECT/OBJET: <u>Proofreading Final Text (English)</u>

The final text will be ready late today for complete final proofreading. I will be distributing approximately 25 pages to each proofreader as soon as the text becomes available.

Please be prepared to stay late (until approximately 10:30 p.m.). Food will be available in the office. Thanks for your help and continuing understanding.

If you have any difficulty in being available, please Advise Valerie at extension 512.

Distribution List
Joanne Rae   Paul Yakabuski
Geoff Craven   Lou Parai
Fruji Bull   Marion Staples
Shelley-Ann Clark   Michael Tiger
Gail Belanger
Meriel Bradford
John Curtis
Ian Currie
Jack Elliott
Ray Labrosse
Bob Martin

APPENDIX "B"

Performance Review

Of Shelley Ann Clark

By

Germain Denis

NON-ROTATIONAL PERFORMANCE REVIEW AND EMPLOYEE APPRAISAL
EXAMEN DU RENDEMENT ET RAPPORT D'APPRÉCIATION DES EMPLOYÉ(E)S NON PERMUTANT(E)S

A. BASIC DATA

I request to have my appraisal report completed in the following official language
Je demande que mon rapport d'évaluation soit préparé dans la langue officielle suivante

☐ French / Français ☒ English / Anglais

Full Name/Nom/Prénom(s)	SIN/NAS	Branch/Division/Section/Mission
CLARK, Shelley Ann	4 3 9 0 6 9 5 0 1	TNO

Classification of employee Classification de l'employé(e)	of position du poste	Date appointed to position Date de nomination au poste	
SCY (4)		April 1986	

Period covered by appraisal/Période d'évaluation From De D/J M Y/A	to/à D/J M Y/A	Position Title/Titre du poste	Position Number Numéro du poste
0 1 0 4 8 6	3 1 1 0 8 7		

Purpose of Appraisal/Motif du rapport

Annual/Annuel ☒ Probationary/Stage ☐ Transfer of employee/Mutation de l'employé(e) ☐ Transfer of Supervisor/Mutation du superviseur ☐ Other (Specify)/Autre (Précisez) ☐

Supervisors since last appraisal/Superviseurs depuis la dernière évaluation

Name/Nom	Period Covered/Période visée	Division/Direction
DENIS, Germain A.	SAME AS ABOVE to/à	TNO
Name/Nom	to/à	

B. CERTIFICATIONS/ATTESTATIONS

Supervisor/Superviseur

I have discussed this report with the employee and believe it to be a fair representation of his/her performance.
J'ai discuté du contenu du présent rapport d'appréciation avec l'employé(e) et je crois qu'il constitue une évaluation juste de son rendement.

Signature _____ Date 1 Dec 87

Reviewing officer/Agent de révision

Comments/Commentaires

Signature _Shelley Ann Clark_ Date Dec. 1/87

Employee/Employé(e)

I have read and discussed this report with my supervisor.
J'ai lu et examiné le présent rapport avec mon superviseur.

☐ Yes/Oui ☐ No/Non

Signature _____ Date _____

I disagree/Je suis en désaccord ☐ comments:/commentaires: ☐ To Follow/Suivront ☐ Attached/Attachés ☐

APPRAISAL REVIEW COMMITTEE/COMITÉ DE RÉVISION DES ÉVALUATIONS

Signature _____ Date 3/12/87
Secretary, Appraisal Review Committee
Secrétaire, Comité d'examen des appréciations

BXT 1097

C. DUTIES AND OBJECTIVES *

1. Co-ordination, processing review of all incoming and outgoing correspondence, Memoranda to Cabinet, (MC's), Travel Authorizations and Travel Expense Claims for signature of the Assistant Chief Negotiator by:

   - Analyzing content for priority and issue sensitivity;
   - Identifying what action is required;
   - Ensuring requested actions are acted upon;
   - Maintaining quality control on all outgoing material;
   - Drafting correspondence;
   - Screening incoming ministerial correspondence to determine priority, responsibility centre, etc.;
   - Editing in both official languages;
   - Establishing and operating response control systems.

2. Communication

   Maintaining good communications with officers of all sector heads by:

   - Maintaining sufficient familiarity with major issues before Assistant Chief Negotiators (ACN);
   - Coordinating information;
   - Establishing good communication channels at all levels;
   - Communicating and interpreting instructions of ACN to others;
   - Interpreting and presenting concerns of others to the ACN.

3. Acts as point of enquiry by Minister's staff, departmental offices, private industry, press, M.P.'s etc. by:

   - Exercising good judgement & initiative;
   - Identifying problem areas;
   - Maintaining up-to-date information.

4. Develops administrative systems and procedures to ensure high volume of documents and correspondence flows smoothly on time by:

- Determining procedures;
- Ensuring procedures are followed;
- Evolving procedures to meet new demands;
- Continuously liaising with all sectors of TNO;
- Guiding & assisting other secretaries in TNO in following these Systems and procedures;

5. <u>Supervisory Skills</u>

From time to time, she liaised, on my behalf with a large number of TNO staff and supervised the assembly of complex Briefing Books for the negotiating sessions.

6. <u>Overseeing Proof Readers</u>

She was also responsible for overseeing the proof readers in charge the printing of the FTA into a booklet form and ensuring that no unauthorized changes were made.

D. RESULTS ACHIEVED

1. All duties were fulfilled speedily, effectively and cheerfully frequently under conditions of extreme pressure. She wrote the TNO guidelines & procedures for submitting MC's to Ministers and coordinated their preparation. She organized complex travel programs and agendas for large groups of people on very short notice in such a way that professional staff were able to concentrate fully on the issues at hand. In so doing, she displayed very considerable resourcefulness and initiative in severe conditions. For example, she organized the travel, etc. for approximately 35 officers to Washington when

the TNO talks were suddenly renewed at 10 p.m. on the night of October 1.

2. She excelled and clearly was highly motivated at being at the communications centre in a continuously evolving environment. She maintained good rapport with sector heads and ensured that information flowed back and forth effectively, efficiently, without delay. For example, she prepared summary reports of events that went on in TNO in my absence that were extremely useful. Her role was widely recognized even by people outside the TNO as evidenced by a number of requests channeled to her to obtain authoritative information on various administrative matters.

3. She handled enquiries from all levels from the Prime Minister's office down with good tact and judgemen t and with considerable resourcefulness. For example, when the morning after the signature of the Free Trade Agreement in Washington on October 4, the Prime Minister's office called to get the original of the Trade Agreement for tabling in the House in 45 minutes, she had to obtain it discreetly from me while a background press briefing was being given to reporters by senior TNO members.

4. Under challenging and always evolving circumstances, she kept documents and correspondence flowing smoothly on schedule. In particular, she supervised the physical preparation of a number of complex briefing books for the main negotiating sessions between Canadian and USA Chief Negotiators and for the Parliamentary Committee on Free Trade. These were always prepared with expertise, reliability and on time.

She also has a very sound knowledge of government procedures, rules and regulations. For example, because of her concerns about events which had implications for document security at TNO she initiated enquiries which led to the discovery of a major security flaw with the first computer system installed in the early days of TNO that resulted in management taking the necessary steps to remove the system and bring in another.

5. These were done professionally, accurately and deadlines were always met. She had a team that respected her line of command and worked well with her.

6. She did her job well and used good judgement when for example, a problem arose over an incorrect words, she took the necessary steps to ensure that it was not changed without obtaining prior approval by authorized officials.

7. Overall, Mrs. Clark operated well above the level of performance normally expected. Her abilities to organize and operate under extreme pressures are unusual and impressive. She is also well experienced in matters of protocol, organizing large meetings and in arranging hospitality.

She would be well suited to a position in the administrative service in an Embassy or in the Protocol Division handling conferences should one become available.

---

* **N.B. Please note that for purposes of clarity pages 1-4 are replicas of the originals that have been retyped in a larger font. The cover page is an original. The originals of the complete document are available for viewing upon request by sending an e-mail to:**

shelleyann.clark3@gmail.com.

APPENDIX "C"

List of Meetings

Between Germain Denis

And the

Canadian Provincial Representatives

LIST OF MEETINGS BETWEEN

GERMAIN DENIS AND THE PROVINCES

N.B. All information was extracted from
Appointment Book kept for Germain Denis
by S.A. Clark

. Attached are photocopies of the original pages

----

1. **TUESDAY, JUNE 9, 1987**

   One on one with Ed Shaske (ALBERTA)

2. **WEDNESDAY, JUNE 10, 1987**

   One on One
   Paul Haddow (Representative for Art Wakabayuskie
   SASKATCHEWAN

3. **WEDNESDAY, JUNE 17, 1987**

   Provincial Briefing (G.A. Denis)
   QUEBEC

4. **TUESDAY, JUNE 23, 1987**

   Provincial Briefing (G.A. Denis)
   Free Trade Negotiations Office - 17th floor-
   Boardroom 'C

5. **TUESDAY, JUNE 30, 1987**

   One on One Provincial Briefing:
   Art Wakabayouki and Paul Haddow, SASKATCHEWAN

6. **THURSDAY, JULY 16, 1987**

   Provincial Briefing (G.A. Denis)
   Free Trade Negotiations Office -17th Floor
   Boardroom 'C'

7. **MONDAY, JULY 27, 1987**

   Federal-Provincial meeting on Agriculture (G.A. Denis)
   Location: Delta Hotel, Algonquin Room, OTTAWA

.../2

- 2 -

8.   **TUESDAY, JULY 28, 1987**

     Meeting with SASKATCHEWAN on CROWN CORPORATIONS
     AND SUBSIDY ISSUES (G.A. Denis)   - Free Trade Negotiations
Office   - 17th floor - Boardroom C

9.   **THURSDAY, JULY 30, 1987**

     Federal-Provincial meeting on SERVICES and SUBSIDIES
     Free Trade Negotiations Office - 17th floor- Boardroom C

10. **THURSDAY, AUGUST 13, 1987**

     Provincial Briefing (G.A. Denis)
     Free Trade Negotiations Office - 17th floor - Boardroom C

11. **MONDAY, AUGUST 31, 1987**

     One on One with Ed Shaske
     ALBERTA

12. **FRIDAY, SEPTEMBER 11, 1987**

     Provincial Briefing (G.A. Denis)
     Free Trade Negotiations Office - 17th floor - Boardroom C

13. **WEDNESDAY, NOVEMBER 4, 1987**

     One on One with Ed Shaske
     ALBERTA

14. **FRIDAY, NOVEMBER 6, 1987**

     One on One with Paul Haddow
     SASKATCHEWAN

15. **WEDNESDAY, DECEMBER 16, 1987**

     Provincial Briefing   (G.A. Denis)
     Sydney, Nova Scotia

.../3

- 3 -

16. **MONDAY, JANUARY 18, 1987**

    One on One with Ed Shaske
    ALBERTA

17. **TUESDAY, JANUARY 26, 1988**

    Provincial Briefing (G.A. Denis)
    QUEBEC
    Location: Chateau Frontenac "Petit Salon"

APPENDIX "D"

Letter from Legal Counsel

To the

Canadian, Prime Minister Brian Mulroney

HAROLD C. FUNK
Barrister & Solicitor

May 26, 1993

The Right Honourable
Brian Mulroney
Prime Minister
of Canada

To all Premiers
of Canada

RE: North American Free Trade Agreement

Dear Prime Minister and Premiers:

I enclose herein the following material.

1.   A letter from the Public Service Alliance of Canada dated July
29, 1988 addressed to my client Shelley Ann Clark from Mary W.
Ramsay, Service Officer together with its contents.

(a)   A chronology of events pages 1 to 11.

(b)   Background information AI-1 through to AI-9 with
      particular interest to pages AI-5, AI-6, and AI-7 to be
      read in conjunction with the tape enclosed herein.

(c)   A performance review of Shelley Ann Clark dated December
      1, 1987.

(d)   Documentation re: Transfer Request of my client.

(e)   An article of the Ottawa Citizen dated March 29, 1989.

I also enclose herein a tape of my conversation with my client
with regard to the procedures that were followed with regard to the
preparation of the briefing books for the main negotiating
sessions, for the North American Free Trade Agreement, and the
procedures that were followed with regard to the doctoring of these
briefing books prior to their being distributed to the Provincial
Representatives for their briefing by Germain Denis, and the
ultimate disposal of these briefing books by Mr. Germain Denis.

Unit 1A, 3205 Swansea Crescent, Ottawa, Ontario K1G 3W5
Tel.: (613) 739-0884   Fax: (613) 739-4673

I would hope that the representatives in the provinces made complete notes of these meetings which can be checked with the briefing books held in the Archives in Ottawa. I would hope that you would check these notes with the briefing books.

I would bring to your attention that the same tactics that were used in this case, are the same as those used in the Constitutional negotiations.

I would be interested in your comments.

Yours Very Truly,

Harold C. Funk

HCF/ck
encls.
c.c. Commissioner
     Norman Inkster
     Royal Canadian
     Mounted Police
     1200 Vanier Parkway
     Ottawa, Ontario
     K1A 0R4

c.c. Leader of the Official
     Opposition Party
     Jean Chretien

c.c. Leader of the New
     Democratic Party
     Audrey McLaughlin

c.c. The Ottawa Citizen
     ATTN: Bert Hill
     ATTN: Dave Brown
     1101 Baxter Road
     Ottawa, Ontario
     K2C 3M4

c.c. CJOH TV
     ATTN: Charlie Greenwell
     Box 5813
     Merivale Depot
     Ottawa, Ontario
     K2C 3G6

3

c.c. Global Television
     ATTN: Editor

c.c. Globe and Mail

c.c. Hon. Don R. Getty
     Premier of Alberta
     Legislative Building
     Edmonton, Alberta
     T5K 2B6

c.c. Hon. Mike Harcourt
     Premier of British Columbia
     Parliament Buildings
     Victoria, B.C.
     V8V 1X4

c.c. Hon. Gary Filmon
     Premier of Manitoba
     204 Legislative Building
     Winnipeg, Manitoba
     R3C 0V8

c.c. Hon Frank McKenna
     Premier of New Brunswick
     Legislative Assembly Building
     P.O. Box 6000
     Federicton, N.B.
     E3B 5H1

c.c. Hon. Donald W. Cameron
     Premier of Nova Scotia
     Province House
     P.O. Box 726
     Halifax, Nova Scotia
     B3J 2T3

c.c. Hon. Bob Rae
     Premier of Ontario
     Room 281
     Legislative Building
     Queen's Park
     Toronto, Ontario
     M7A 1A5

c.c. Hon. Joseph A. Ghiz
     Premier of Prince Edward Island
     122 North River Road
     Charlottetown, P.E.I.
     C1A 3K8

4

c.c. Hon. Robert Bourassa
     Premier of Quebec
     Edifice J.
     3rd Floor
     885 Grande Allee East
     Quebec
     G1A 1A2

c.c. Hon Roy Romanow
     Premier of Saskatchewan
     Legislative Building
     2405 Legislative Drive
     Regina, Saskatchewan
     S4S 0B3

c.c. Hon Clyde Wells
     Premier of Newfoundland
     Confederation Building
     P.O. Box 8700
     St. John's, Newfoundland
     A1B 4J6

APPENDIX "E"

Canadian

House of Commons Debates/

"HANSARD"

Dated January 20, 1994

CANADA

House of Commons Debates

VOLUME 133　　•　　NUMBER 100　　•　　1st SESSION　　•　　35th PARLIAMENT

OFFICIAL REPORT
(HANSARD)

January 20, 1994

Speaker: The Honourable Gilbert Parent

against the Crown like anybody else. It so happens he had brought an action against the government, exercising a right we all have.

Any of us who risked sustaining damage or injury on federal property due to the negligence of a government employee would be entitled to sue the Crown. Anybody, including me, any Minister and the Leader of the Opposition. But, to avoid controversy, the Minister has decided to withdraw his appeal. If his counsel did not carry out these instructions—and if he is watching today, he can see that the Minister of Revenue agrees—he should have carried out his instructions to the letter.

* * *

[*English*]

TRADE

Mrs. Diane Ablonczy (Calgary North): Mr. Speaker, my question is for the Minister for International Trade.

A woman by the name of Shelley Anne Clark who is an employee of the federal government has publicly made serious accusations concerning the free trade agreement, including a statement that the actual text of the agreement has never been disclosed. She says that the real agreement contains terms which limit Canada's sovereignty over our resources.

On behalf of Canadians who have called me and other MPs to find out whether this is true, would the minister lay the matter to rest today by stating conclusively that the text of the free trade agreement which has been made public is in fact the true and complete agreement?

Hon. Roy MacLaren (Minister for International Trade): Mr. Speaker, the allegations made by the Shelley Anne Clark were investigated by the previous government and found to be unwarranted. Our practices regarding privacy of information would preclude me from commenting any further on her allegations.

Mrs. Diane Ablonczy (Calgary North): Mr. Speaker, could the minister state conclusively that the text of the agreement which has been made public is in fact the true and complete text? That is what people want to know.

● (1440)

Hon. Roy MacLaren (Minister for International Trade): Mr. Speaker, the text made available by the previous government is, in my understanding, the actual text.

* * *

[*Translation*]

TOBACCO TAXES

Mr. Pierre Brien (Témiscamingue): Mr. Speaker, my question is for the Minister of National Revenue. While the Liberal ministers have fun passing the buck on the cigarette smuggling

issue, the Premier of Quebec has said once again that he intends to lower the tax to curb the problem.

Is the Minister prepared to acknowledge that one of the best ways of eliminating smuggling is by reducing the excessive tax? And how does the minister feel about the Quebec Premier's proposed course of action?

Right Hon. Jean Chrétien (Prime Minister): Mr. Speaker, I discussed this matter with the Premier of Quebec in December and discussions are under way with other governments at this time. We intend to take the necessary steps to curb smuggling as soon as possible.

Mr. Pierre Brien (Témiscamingue): My supplemental is for the Prime Minister as he appears to have taken over question period this afternoon.

Will the Prime Minister concede that as a result of high taxes, the federal treasury has lost nearly $600 million, according to the Finance Department's 1992 estimates alone, and that as a result of this, smokers contribute considerably less to the health care system?

Right Hon. Jean Chrétien (Prime Minister): Mr. Speaker, there is no question that governments have lost a considerable amount of money. That is why we have decided to consult with the provinces and work together with them to address the smuggling problem. If both levels of government cannot co-operate, if one acts and the other does not, then we will not get the hoped-for results. We are working right now to achieve a consensus on an effective way of curbing smuggling.

* * *

[*English*]

ABORIGINAL AFFAIRS

Mr. Chuck Strahl (Fraser Valley East): Mr. Speaker, my question is for the Minister of Indian Affairs and Northern Development.

The minister is quoted in yesterday's Toronto *Sun* as saying that the government will have plans for native self-government in place within six months.

Could the minister tell the members of the House and the people of Canada, indeed the aboriginal people themselves precisely what is meant by self-government?

Hon. Ron Irwin (Minister of Indian Affairs and Northern Development): Mr. Speaker, yesterday I announced a process of six months of discussions with the provinces, the territories and the regional and provincial governments to assist the implementation of the inherent right of self-government which this government is committed to.

In answer to my hon. friend's question, it is a three-in-one formula: self-determination, self-sufficiency and self-government within one Canada. We intend to proceed with fairness and in the healing process in the end we will have a better country.

APPENDIX "F"

Guest Speaking Engagement in

Vancouver's

Robson Square Media Centre

June 25, 1994

The "national" media won't touch them

GLEN KEALEY

Kealey is the former Hull area commercial developer who exposed the system of organised crime run by Mulroney's government and the complicity of the R.C.M.P. and justice system.

In 1986 Kealey was asked for a bribe by Public Works Minister Roch LaSalle, who offered him government support for his project in exchange for 5% of all government contributions on top of the $5,000 up front. Investigating, Kealey found evidence of a massive bribe and kickback scheme operated and controlled right out of the P.M.O., and a close collaboration between the Tories, the media, and police. Kealey successfully charged 13 people, including members of the government and R.C.M.P, with criminal conspiracy.

Clark was the civil servant working on the U.S.-Canada Free Trade Agreement who was called to work between midnight and 4 am beginning January 1987 and ordered to falsify, then eventually shred, briefing papers designed to mislead provincial premiers about what was in the F.T.A.. Clark says the deal's implementing scheme has never been made public, and that it contains plans for Quebec's separation, massive water diversion, and absorption into the U.S. by the year 2005. After being abandoned by her union and threatened by secret service, Clark went public with her story in May 1993 and ran as a National Party candidate in the election. Canada's media monopoly would rather have you think about O.J. Simpson.

SHELLEY ANN CLARK

The lawyers won't sue them
The politicians pass laws to
gag them . . . But still the story gets out.

Hear them in person

Sat. June 25, 1994   7 p.m.
Conference Theatre #3
Robson Square Media Centre
800 Robson St. $10 donation

Canadian Institute for Political Integrity (CIPI) Box 1634, Stn B, Hull, Que. J8X 3K5 (819) 778-1705; fax (613) 747-1644
B.C. Chapter: 352-6369 • in Vancouver: 739-7985

APPENDIX "G"

National Party of Canada

Federal Election Campaign Flyer

Candidate: Shelley Ann Clark

1993 Federal Elections

Candidate For Carleton/Gloucester

National Party of Canada / Parti National du Canada

**Biography of
Shelley Ann Clark
Candidate For Carleton/Gloucester
National Party of Canada/Parti National Du Canada**

Shelley Ann Clark was born and educated in Ottawa. Shortly after graduating from business college in 1961, she joined the Department of External Affairs. Aside from 11 years' "Motherhood Leave", her entire career was associated with this Department, although she was frequently on loan to foreign governments. The assignments resulted from her competence with protocol, public relations and administration. Her first book was,"How to Become a Professional in the Office". She also wrote an instruction manual based on her experience; reportedly it is still in use. She also served as a guestspeaker and as a panelist in radio debates. A frequent issue was "Honesty in Government". She has a proven record in this area.

Shelley Ann Clark is an avowed anti-corruptionist. She does not tolerate the theft of public resources by people entrusted with high office. She never sold her silence for a share of the loot. Perhaps the most noteworthy example was her reaction when she discovered that diplomats were systematically looting the fragile economy of a central African nation.

She did not ask for "hush-money". Instead she launched an investigation and played a major role in the arrest and subsequent conviction of the ring leader. Shelley Ann Clark will not remain silent in the shadow of corruption.

The current issue,"Free Trade", is by far the most significant in her remarkable career. As a Free Trade official during the recent negotiations between Canada and the USA, she became aware of astounding misrepresentations made to the Provincial Premiers, along with the unauthorized shredding or covert disappearance of key documents.

Shelley Ann Clark stands for **Integrity, Freedom of Speech, Freedom of the Press and Freedom of Choice**. She is approachable. She will listen to your concerns.

Authorized by the official
agent Margaret R. Bowlby
for Shelley Ann Clark
Carleton/Gloucester
195 Lennox St.
733-3033

CLARK Shelley Ann	X

APPENDIX "H"

Letter to the

Honourable Roy MacLaren

Dated June 5, 1994

**Canadian
Institute for
Political
Integrity**

P.O. Box 1634
Station B.
Hull, Quebec. J8X 3X5

June 5, 1994

Telephone: (819) 778 1705
Facsimile: (613) 747-1644

The Honourable Roy MacLaren
Minister for International Trade
Department of Foreign Affairs &
  International Trade Canada
Ottawa, Ontario

FAX: (613) 996-8924 / 995-8359

Dear Minister,

Canada/U.S.A. Free Trade Agreement

INTEGRITY

As you are already aware, I, Shelley Ann Clark disclosed
the treasonous acts surrounding the rigging of the Canada/U.S.A.
Free Trade Agreement (FTA). Ever since I disclosed to my union,
the Public Service Alliance of Canada, in July 1988, I have been
severely harassed by those in charge of the previous government and
officials in the Department of Foreign Affairs. At present, I will
not go into details of the harassment except to say that it began
in the spring of 1989. These details were carefully documented,
with copies given to appropriate officials.

This letter deals only with harassment from January 1994
onward which has been directed upon my person. The following
actions, taken by the Department of Foreign Affairs, are totally
unacceptable.

1) The Department of Foreign Affairs reportedly assigned a Mr.
    Michael Conway to my case. Mr. Conway, immediately after his
    appointment, contacted my immediate supervisor, Mr. Marius
    Bujold and detailed my activities, including a transcript of
    an Alberta talk show where I had been the guest. In addition
    he demanded that Mr. Bujold carry your Department's messages
    to me (as stated previously in my April 16, 1994 letter to
    you). Mr. Conway has created an extremely difficult working
    environment for my supervisor and me. Under those conditions,
    I ask you Mr. Minister, how can my immediate supervisor be
    expected to remain impartial towards me? The entire situation
    created in the workplace by Michael Conway is intolerable. In
    my view, my supervisor should have been left out of this
    situation altogether. This would· have engendered a more
    productive working relationship between us.

/2

- 2 -

2) As stated in the aforementioned letter, the Department of Foreign Affairs has twice threatened me with dismissal. On the second occasion I was told that the next warning would definitely be in writing and could result in my immediate dismissal. This is mental cruelty; I am sole provider for my family and these people are aware of this. They are forcing me to work under the constant threat of dismissal, along with the probability of never being employed in Ottawa in the future.

3) For the Department to have relocated Germain Denis (the same person I accused of sexual and general harassment — let alone his misdeeds involving the FTA), along with his entire branch to a work space adjoining my own, in Tower B-4 of the Lester B. Pearson building, is beyond contempt.

Mr. Minister, I plead with you to take immediate action to end this ongoing harassment being directed by the Department against me. I am a Canadian who did what I firmly believe is in the best interest of Canada and Canadians. I should not be punished solely for "doing my duty".

Sincerely,

Shelley Ann Clark

cc: Lloyd Fucile, PSAC

APPENDIX "I"

Response by the

Office of the

Minister for International Trade

Dated June 24, 1994

Minister for International Trade   Ministre du Commerce international

CANADA

JUN 24 1994

Ms. Shelley Ann Clark
Canadian Institute for Political Integrity
P. O. Box 1634
Station B
Hull, Quebec.
J8X 3X5

Dear Ms. Clark:

Thank-you for your letter of June 5, 1994 to which I have been asked to reply.

Your letter alleging harassment by the Department of Foreign Affairs and International Trade
has been sent to the Department's Personnel Branch for consideration. Officials from the
Branch will be in touch with you in due course.

Yours sincerely,

Pierre Giroux
Executive Assistant to the
Minister for International Trade

Ottawa, Canada K1A 0G2

FIGHTING SHADOWS

"You can see them, but you can't touch them"
The True Story
Of a Whistleblower
The Aftermath and her Battle for Justice

Shelley Ann Clark

VOLUME II

CPSIA information can be obtained at www.ICGtesting.com
Printed in the USA
LVOW090105300312

275190LV00001B/15/P

9 781465 341396